Tabl

MW01133541

Answer Key in middle of book

Your Body Systems

Your body is made of many systems which work together. These systems work in groups. Use the Word Bank to label the different body systems in each group.

Movement Group

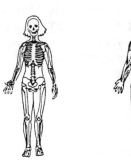

Control Group

 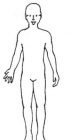 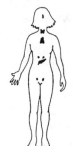

_____   _____   _____   _____   _____

Energy Group

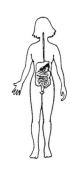 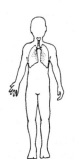 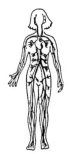 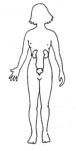

_____   _____   _____   _____

Word Bank

skeletal	muscular	digestive
respiratory	circulatory	urinary
nervous	sensory	endocrine

Your Framework

Label your body's framework with the common name of each bone.

Beneath each write the matching scientific name.

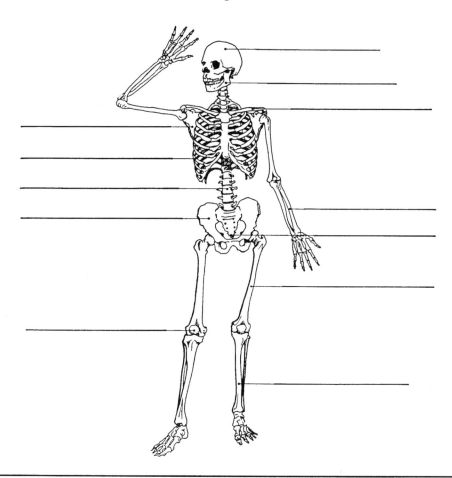

Word Bank
Common Name (Scientific Name)

rib (rib)	shinbone (tibia)
skull (cranium)	collarbone (clavicle)
tailbone (coccyx)	shoulder blade (scapula)
kneecap (patella)	thighbone (femur)
hipbone (pelvis)	lower arm bone (radius)
jawbone (mandible)	backbone (vertebrae)

Your Head Bones

Label these bones that are found in your head and neck.

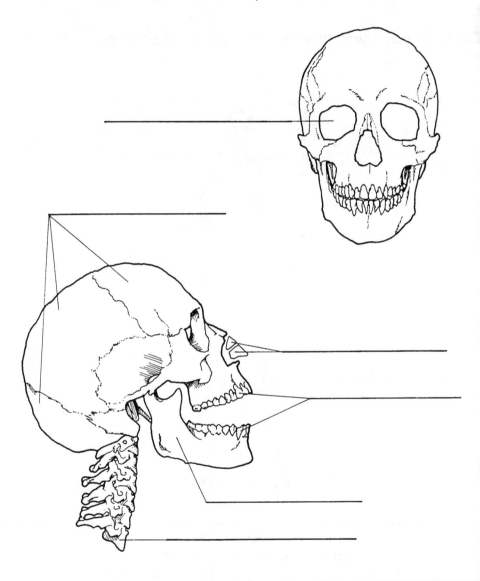

Word Bank

skull bones   eye socket
jawbone (mandible)   nose cartilage
teeth   vertebrae

The Leg Bone's Connected to the Hip Bone

The place where two or more bones meet is called a **joint**. Joints are either movable or immovable. There are four kinds of movable joints: **hinge, pivot, gliding** and **ball-and-socket**. Label each joint on the skeleton below.

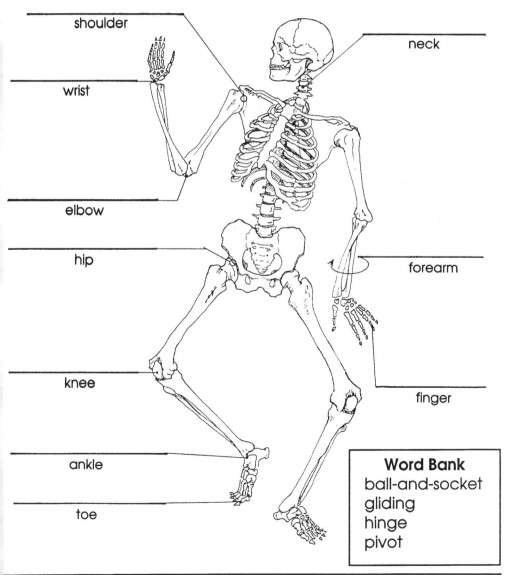

shoulder

neck

wrist

elbow

hip

forearm

knee

finger

ankle

toe

Word Bank
ball-and-socket
gliding
hinge
pivot

Your Bones

Label the parts of the long bone pictured here.

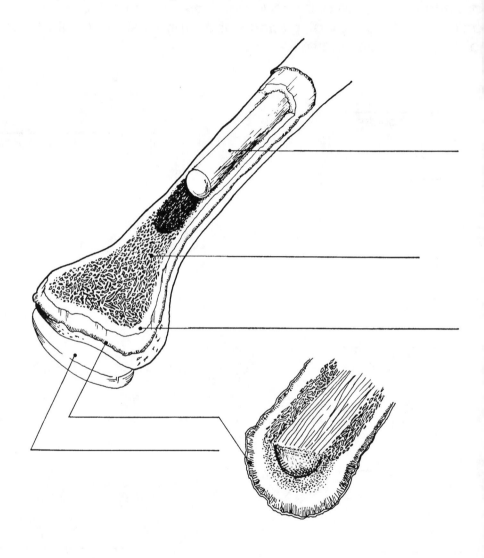

Word Bank

marrow   periosteum
calcified bone   spongy bone
cartilage

Sticks and Stones May Break Your Bones

A break in a bone is called a **fracture**. Some of the common types of fractures are pictured below.

Label the different kinds of fractures.

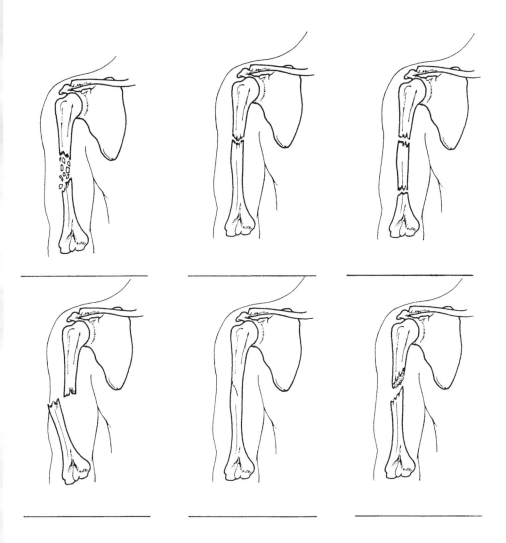

Word Bank

closed fracture	open fracture	multiple fracture
greenstick fracture	comminuted fracture	spiral fracture

Your Backbone

Label the regions of your backbone, or vertebral column.

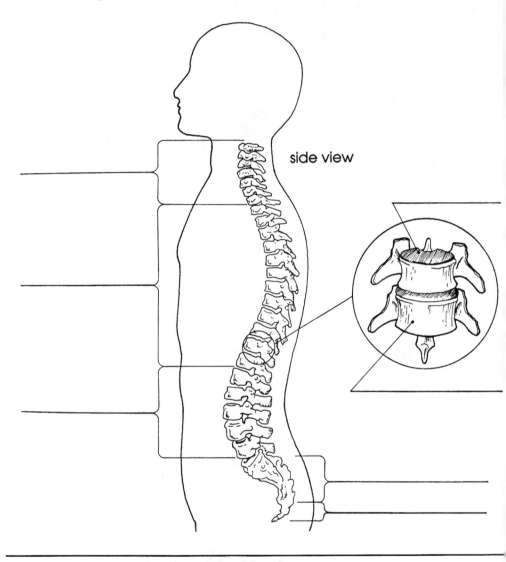

side view

Your Hands and Feet

Label the bones of the hand and foot.

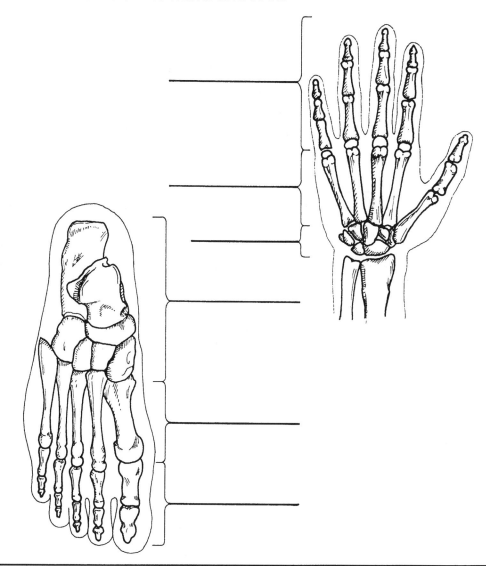

Word Bank
Common Name (Scientific Name)

digits (phalanges)   instep (metatarsals)
wrist (carpals)   digits (phalanges)
ankle (tarsals)   palm (metacarpals)

        IF0226 Human Body

Your Leg Bones

Label the different leg bones and regions.

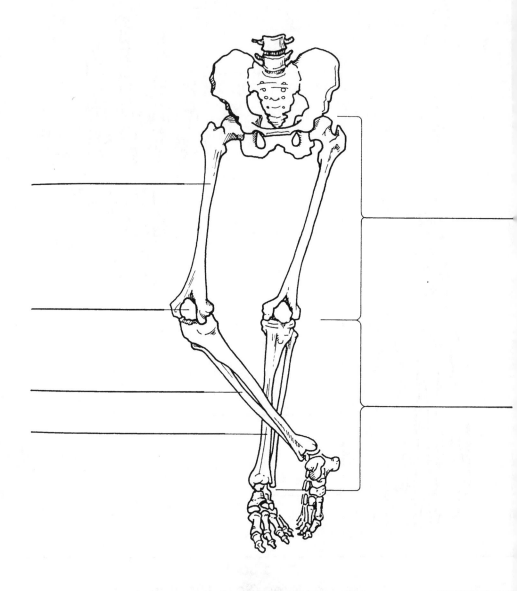

Word Bank

upper leg	tibia	fibula
lower leg	femur	patella

Your Pelvis

The framework of bones that supports the lower part of the abdomen is called the **pelvis**. The male pelvis is heart-shaped and narrow. The female pelvis is much wider and flatter, with a larger central cavity to accomodate a fetus during pregnancy and childbirth.

Label the parts of the pelvis pictured below.

Male Pelvis   **Female Pelvis**

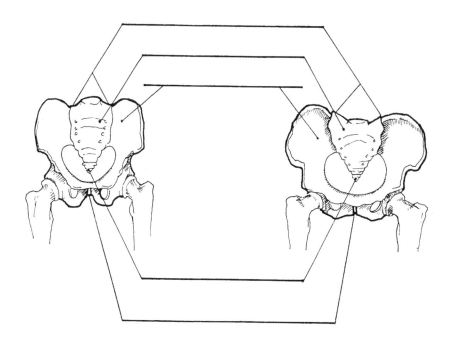

Word Bank

hipbone	sacroiliac joint
interpubic joint	coccyx
sacrum	

Bones of Your Arm

Label the different arm bones and regions.

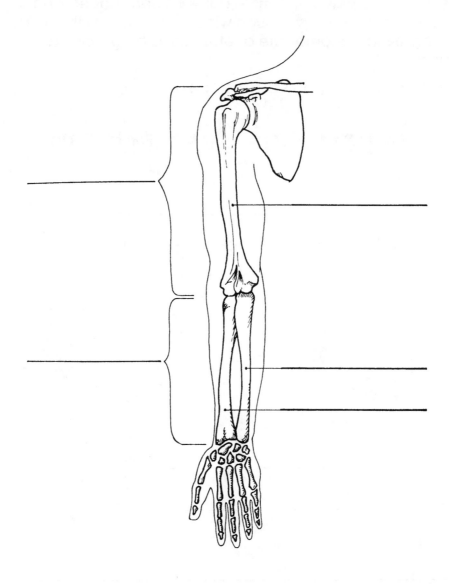

Word Bank

upper arm   ulna   humerus

lower arm   radius

Inside Your Teeth

Your teeth are made up of a number of layers. Label the layers and outside parts of the tooth below.

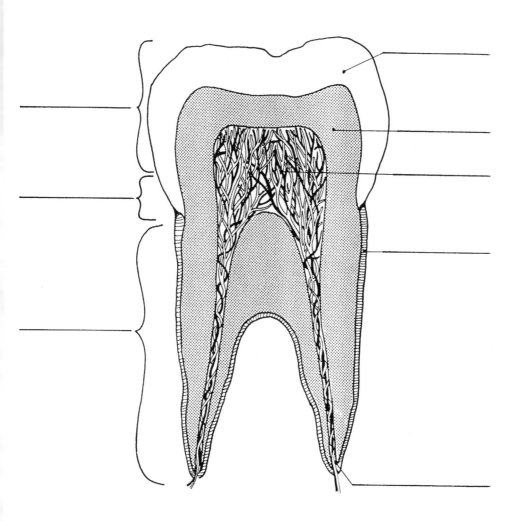

Word Bank

neck	root	crown	dentin
cementum	enamel	pulp	root canal

A Bit About Bites

Each of the pictures on this page illustrates a different **bite**.
The bite is the angle at which the upper and lower teeth meet.

Label the kind of bite found in each left-hand picture. Then draw a line from the bite on the left side of the page to the corresponding profile on the right side.

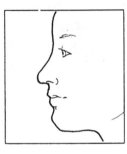

_____

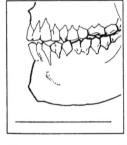

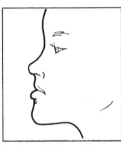

_____

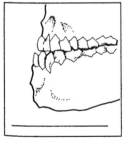

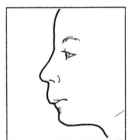

_____

Complete this sentence: "A dentist can correct overbite or

underbite by _____

_____ "
.

Word Bank

overbite   underbite   normal bite

Four Kinds of Teeth

You have four kinds of teeth in your mouth. Label the adult teeth pictured below.

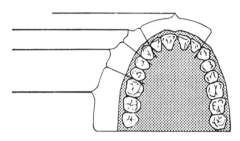

Adult upper

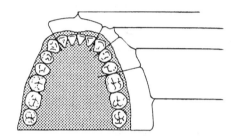

Adult lower

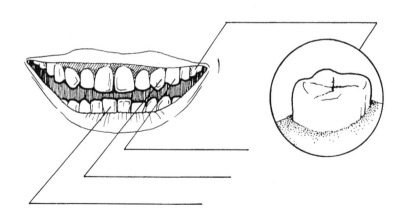

Word Bank

canines   bicuspids   incisors   molars

Bones (Skeletal System Review)

Complete the puzzle.

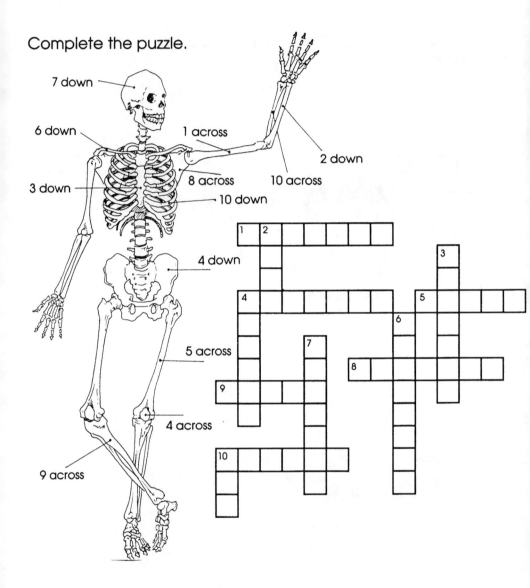

7 down
6 down
3 down
1 across
2 down
8 across
10 across
10 down
4 down
5 across
4 across
9 across

		Word Bank		
femur		pelvis		scapula
ulna		patella		cranium
clavicle		tibia		humerus
radius		rib		sternum

Muscle Man

There are hundreds of muscle groups in your body. Label these muscles that appear on the surface of your body.

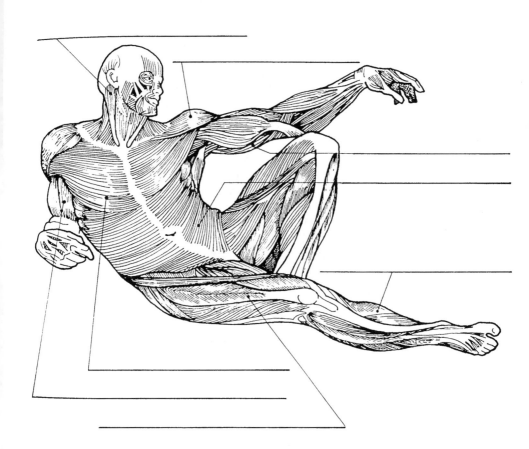

Word Bank
Common Name (Scientific Name)

calf muscles (gastrocnemius)   chest muscles (pectorals)
shoulder muscles (deltoids)   triceps
thigh muscles (quadraceps)   biceps
head muscles (sternocleidomastoids)
stomach muscles (inter coastals)

Skeletal Muscles

Skeletal muscles are attached to the skeleton by means of **tendons**.

Label the parts of the arm pictured below.

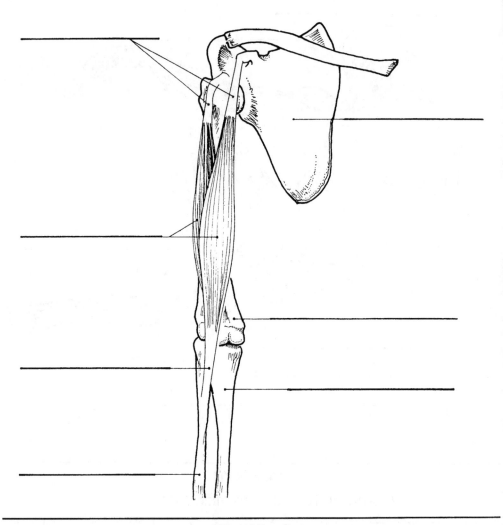

Word Bank

tendons	shoulder blade
biceps muscle	humerus
radius	ulna

Your Muscles

Label the three different kinds of muscles in section **A**. Give an example of the work they do.

Label the muscle parts in section **B**.

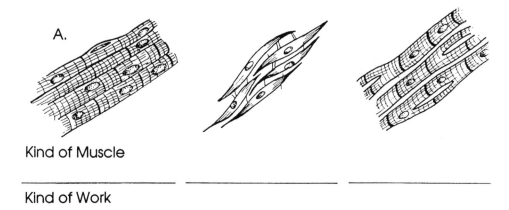

A.

Kind of Muscle

_____ _____ _____

Kind of Work

_____ _____ _____

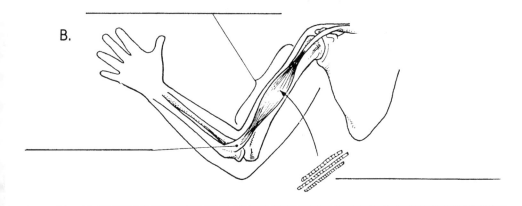

B.

Word Bank

skeletal muscles   tendon
muscle fiber   muscle group
cardiac muscles   smooth muscles

These muscles can make your heart beat.
These muscles can move your bones.
These muscles can move food in your stomach.

Working Pairs

The muscles in both your upper arms and upper legs are very much alike. They both work in pairs to help raise and lower the limbs. Label the parts of these "working pairs."

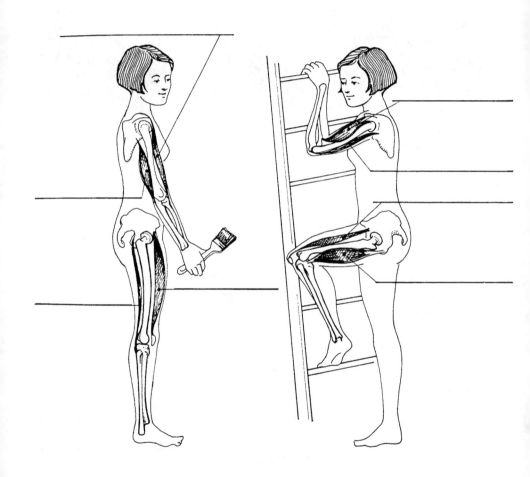

Word Bank

biceps relaxed	biceps contracted
triceps relaxed	triceps contracted
quadriceps relaxed	quadriceps contracted
hamstring relaxed	hamstring contracted

Your Circulatory System

Label the parts of your circulatory system.

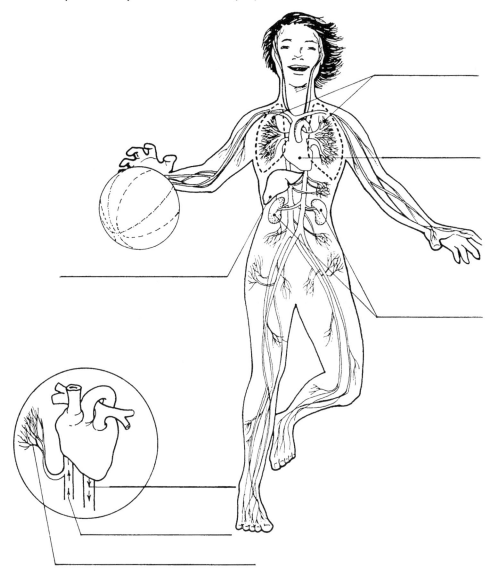

Word Bank

heart	lungs	kidneys
liver	artery	vein
capillaries		

Veins and Arteries

Arteries

Draw red arrows on the arteries showing the flow of blood away from the heart.

Veins

Draw blue arrows on the veins showing the flow of blood back to the heart.

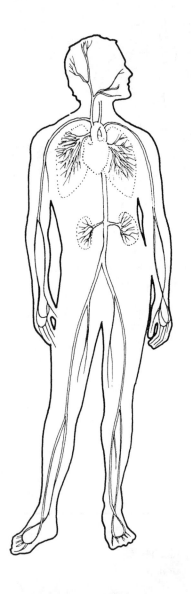

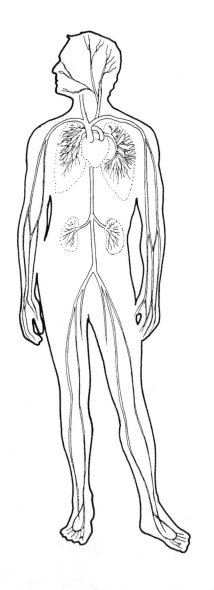

Your Heart

Label the parts of your heart.

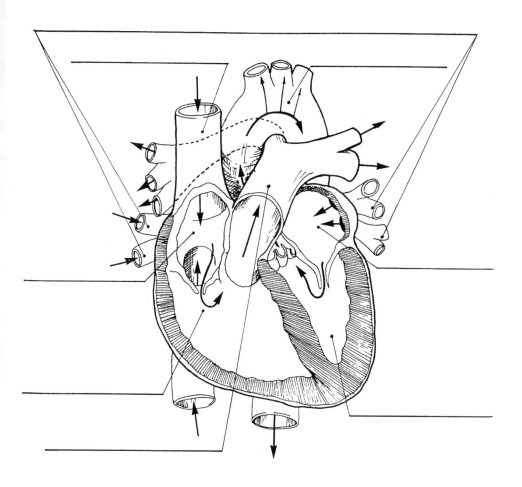

Lub - Dub, Lub - Dub
(Circulatory System Review)

Use the Word Bank
to complete the puzzle.

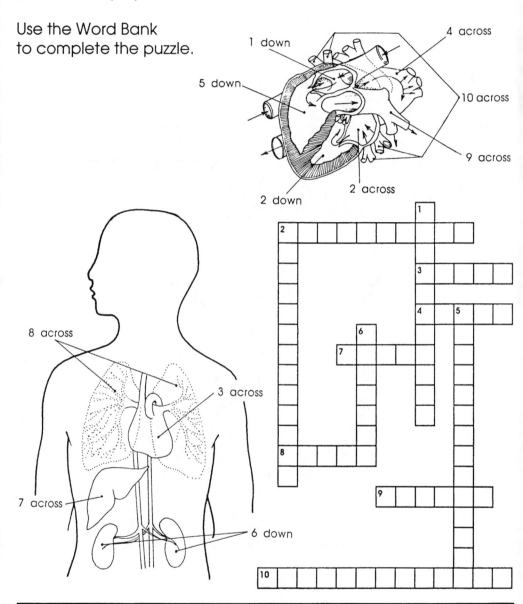

Word Bank

lungs	heart	liver
kidneys	aorta	right atrium
right ventricle	left ventricle	left atrium
pulmonary vein	artery	

Your Respiratory System

Label the parts of your respiratory system.

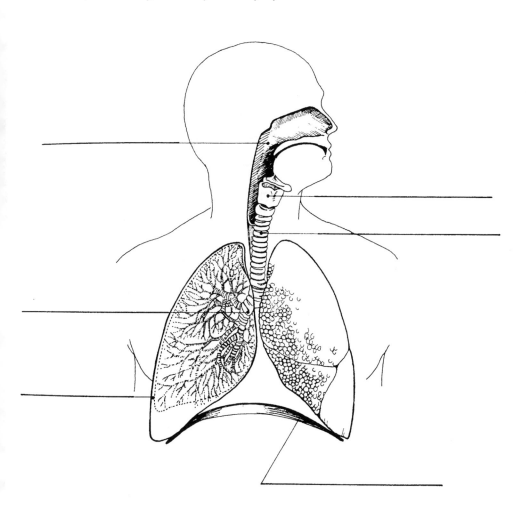

Your Lungs

Label the parts of your lungs.

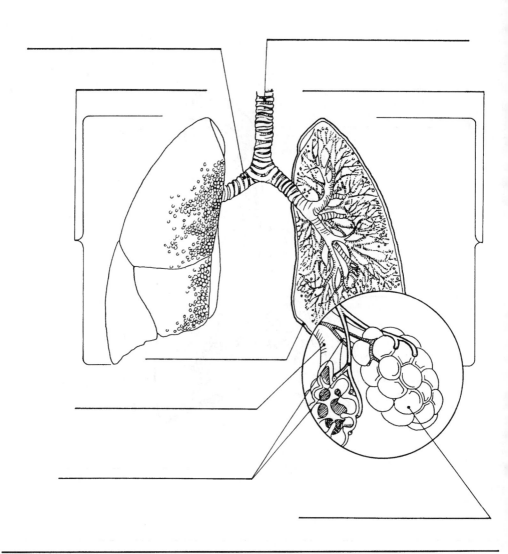

Word Bank

trachea	bronchial tube
pleura	capillaries
bronchiole	alveoli
right lung	left lung

Breathe In! Breathe Out!

You breathe in and breathe out almost 20,000 times each day!
Label these two pictures either **Inhale** (breathe in) or **Exhale**
(breathe out). Label the other parts of your breathing system
using the Word Bank.

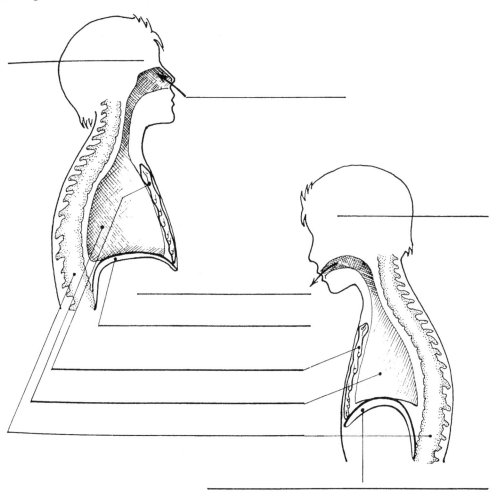

Word Bank

contracted diaphragm   oxygen
carbon dioxide   lung
relaxed diaphragm   spine
breastbone

Huff – Puff (Respiratory System Review)

Use the Word Bank to complete the puzzle.

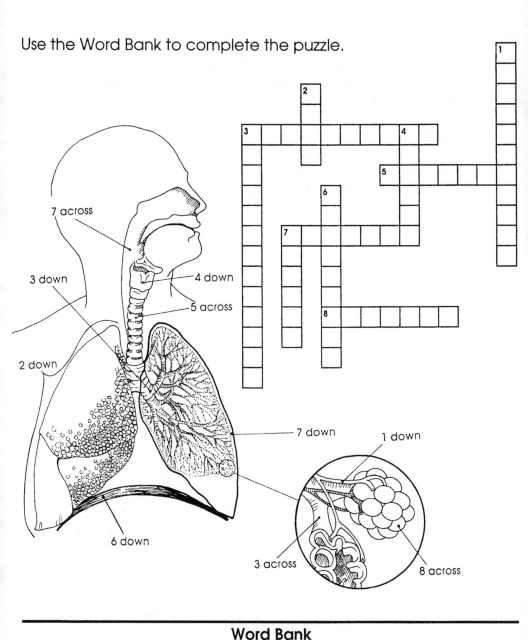

7 across

3 down

4 down

5 across

2 down

7 down

1 down

6 down

3 across

8 across

Word Bank

diaphragm	bronchial tube	trachea
alveoli	lung	larynx
bronchioli	pleura	pharynx
capillaries		

Your Digestive System

Label the parts of your digestive system.

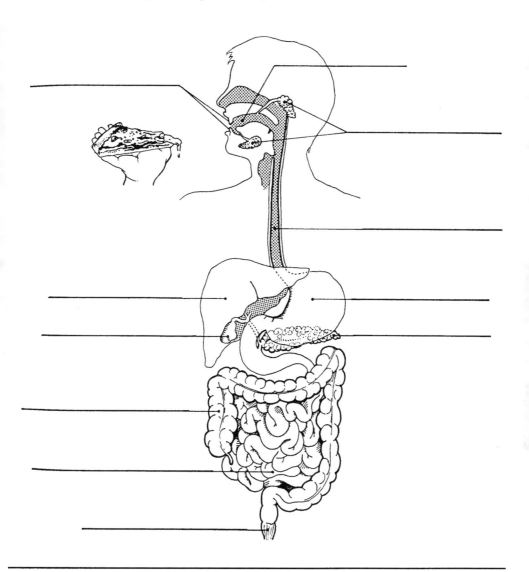

Word Bank

pancreas	liver	gallbladder
stomach	mouth	large intestine
esophagus	teeth	small intestine
salivary glands	anus	

The Alimentary Canal

The main part of the digestive system is the **alimentary canal**, a tube which starts at the mouth, and travels through the body ending at the anus.

Label the parts of the alimentary canal.

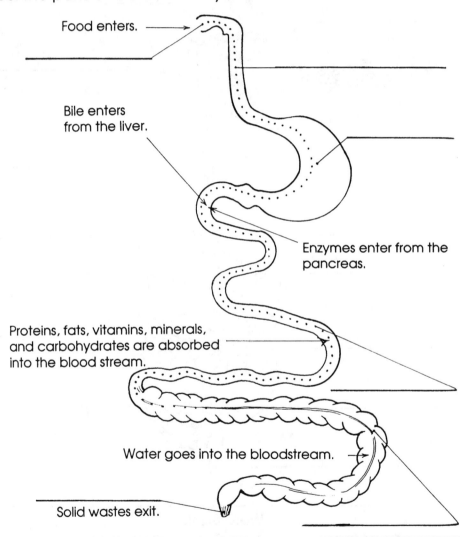

Food enters. —————

Bile enters from the liver.

Enzymes enter from the pancreas.

Proteins, fats, vitamins, minerals, and carbohydrates are absorbed into the blood stream.

Water goes into the bloodstream.

Solid wastes exit.

Word Bank

anus	small intestine	esophagus
mouth	large intestine	stomach

The Stomach

The **stomach** is the widest part of the alimentary canal. The stomach has three layers of muscles which allow it to contract in different directions. The contracting motion mashes food and mixes it with digestive juices.

Label the parts of the stomach and the tubes leading into and out of the stomach.

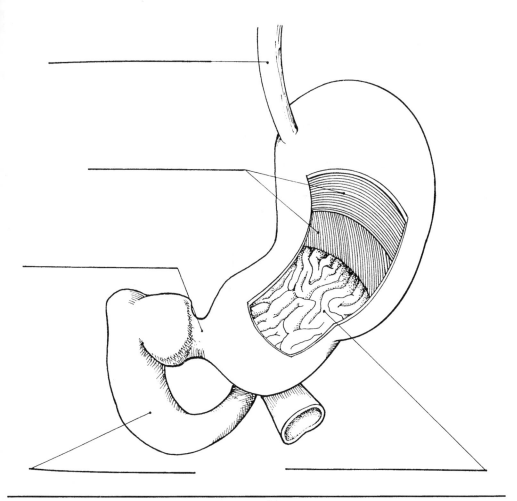

Word Bank

sphincter   duodenum   mucous membrane
muscle layers   esophagus

Digestion in the Mouth

Label the parts of the digestive system located in and around the mouth.

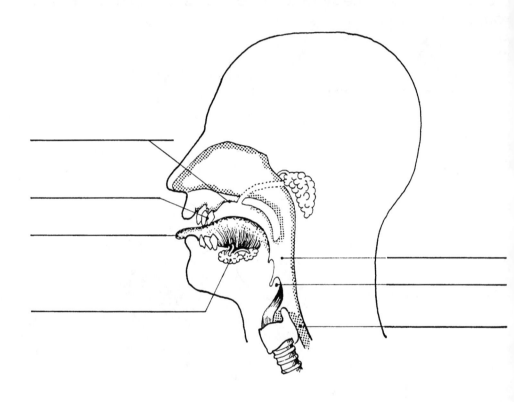

Word Bank

teeth	tongue	palate
epiglottis	esophagus	salivary glands
pharynx		

Digestion Helpers

Label these organs that aid in the digestion of the food you eat.

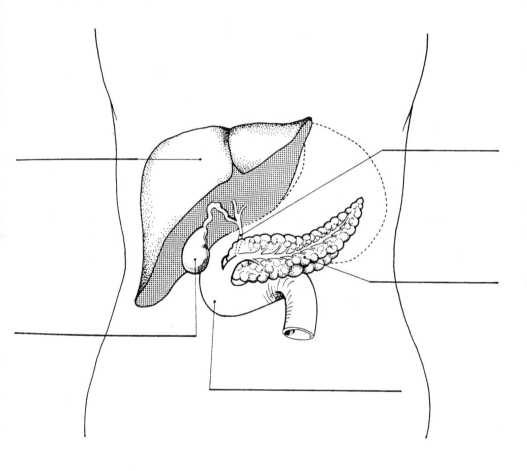

Word Bank

liver   pancreas   gallbladder
bile duct   duodenum

Gulp, Gulp (Digestive System Review)

Use the Word Bank to complete the puzzle.

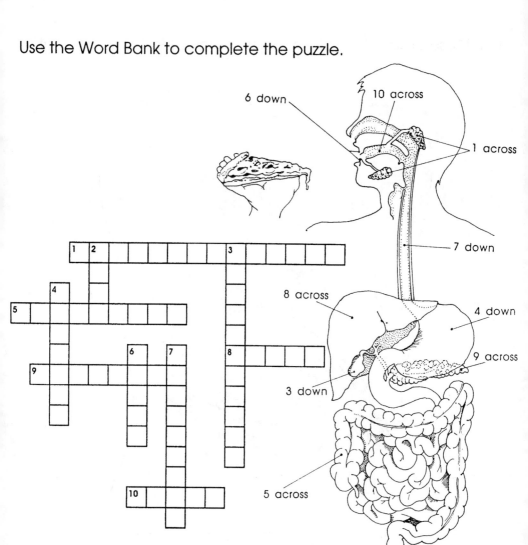

Word Bank

mouth · gall bladder · liver
pancreas · intestine · teeth
salivary glands · esophagus · anus
stomach

Let's Look in Your Mouth!

What do you see when you open your mouth in front of a mirror?
Label the different parts.

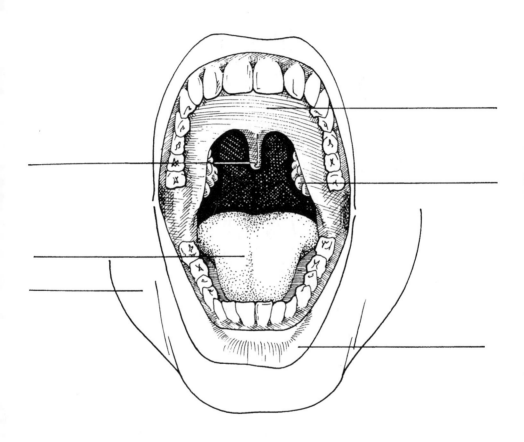

Word Bank

tongue	uvula	cheek
lip	tonsils	palate

Blood Scrubbers

Label the different parts of your body's urinary system.

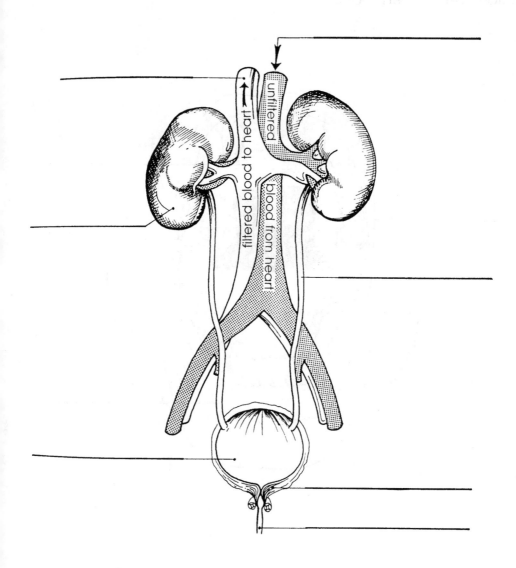

Word Bank

vein	artery	ureter
urethra	bladder	kidney
muscle		

Answer Key
Human Body

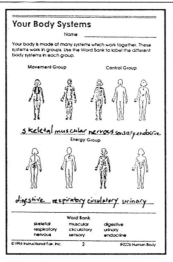

Your Body Systems
Name

Your body is made of many systems which work together. These systems work in groups. Use the Word Bank to label the different body systems in each group.

Movement Group — Control Group

skeletal muscular nervous sensory endocrine

Energy Group

digestive respiratory circulatory urinary

Word Bank

skeletal	muscular	digestive
respiratory	circulatory	urinary
nervous	sensory	endocrine

©1994 Instructional Fair, Inc. 2 IF0226 Human Body

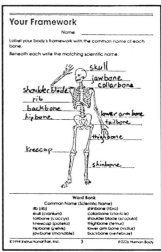

Your Framework
Name

Label your body's framework with the common name of each bone.

Beneath each write the matching scientific name.

skull
jawbone
collarbone
shoulderblade
rib
backbone
hipbone
lower arm bone
tailbone
thighbone
kneecap
shinbone

Word Bank
Common Name (Scientific Name)

rib (rib)	shinbone (tibia)
skull (cranium)	collarbone (clavicle)
tailbone (coccyx)	shoulder blade (scapula)
kneecap (patella)	thighbone (femur)
hipbone (pelvis)	lower arm bone (radius)
jawbone (mandible)	backbone (vertebrae)

©1994 Instructional Fair, Inc. 3 IF0226 Human Body

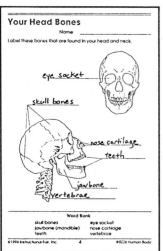

Your Head Bones
Name

Label these bones that are found in your head and neck.

eye socket
skull bones
nose cartilage
teeth
jawbone
vertebrae

Word Bank

skull bones	eye socket
jawbone (mandible)	nose cartilage
teeth	vertebrae

©1994 Instructional Fair, Inc. 4 IF0226 Human Body

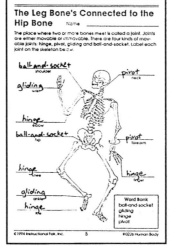

The Leg Bone's Connected to the Hip Bone
Name

The place where two or more bones meet is called a joint. Joints are either movable or immovable. There are four kinds of movable joints: hinge, pivot, gliding and ball-and-socket. Label each joint on the skeleton below.

ball-and-socket shoulder
gliding wrist
hinge elbow
ball-and-socket hip
hinge knee
gliding ankle
hinge toe
pivot neck
pivot forearm
hinge finger

Word Bank
ball-and-socket
gliding
hinge
pivot

©1994 Instructional Fair, Inc. 5 IF0226 Human Body

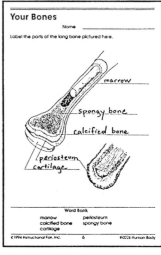

Your Bones
Name

Label the parts of the long bone pictured here.

marrow
spongy bone
calcified bone
periosteum
cartilage

Word Bank

marrow	periosteum
calcified bone	spongy bone
cartilage	

©1994 Instructional Fair, Inc. 6 IF0226 Human Body

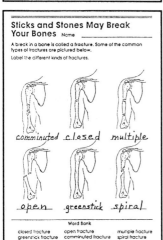

Sticks and Stones May Break Your Bones
Name

A break in a bone is called a fracture. Some of the common types of fractures are pictured below.

Label the different kinds of fractures.

comminuted closed multiple
open greenstick spiral

Word Bank

closed fracture	multiple fracture
greenstick fracture	spiral fracture
open fracture	
comminuted fracture	

©1994 Instructional Fair, Inc. 7 IF0226 Human Body

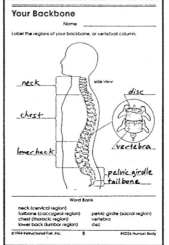

Your Backbone
Name

Label the regions of your backbone, or vertebral column.

side view
neck
disc
chest
vertebra
lower back
pelvic girdle
tailbone

Word Bank

neck (cervical region)	
tailbone (coccygeal region)	pelvic girdle (sacral region)
chest (thoracic region)	vertebra
lower back (lumbar region)	disc

©1994 Instructional Fair, Inc. 8 IF0226 Human Body

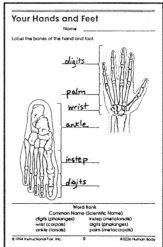

Your Hands and Feet
Name

Label the bones of the hand and foot.

digits
palm
wrist
ankle
instep
digits

Word Bank
Common Name (Scientific Name)

digits (phalanges)	instep (metatarsals)
wrist (carpals)	digits (phalanges)
ankle (tarsals)	palm (metacarpals)

©1994 Instructional Fair, Inc. 9 IF0226 Human Body

Your Leg Bones

Name _____

Label the different leg bones and regions.

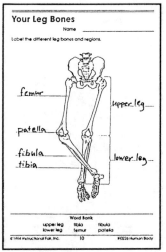

femur

patella

fibula

tibia

upper leg

lower leg

Your Pelvis

Name _____

The framework of bones that supports the lower part of the abdomen is called the pelvis. The male pelvis is heart-shaped and narrow. The female pelvis is much wider and flatter, with a larger central cavity to accomodate a fetus during pregnancy and childbirth.

Label the parts of the pelvis pictured below.

Male Pelvis   Female Pelvis

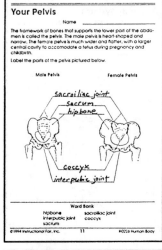

sacroiliac joint

sacrum

hipbone

coccyx

interpubic joint

Bones of Your Arm

Name _____

Label the different arm bones and regions.

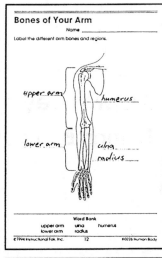

upper arm

lower arm

humerus

ulna

radius

Inside Your Teeth

Name _____

Your teeth are made up of a number of layers. Label the layers and outside parts of the tooth below.

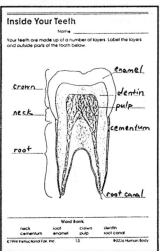

enamel

crown

dentin

pulp

neck

cementum

root

root canal

A Bit About Bites

Name _____

Each of the pictures on this page illustrates a different bite. The bite is the angle at which the upper and lower teeth meet.

Label the kind of bite found in each left-hand picture. Then draw a line from the bite on the left side of the page to the corresponding profile on the right side.

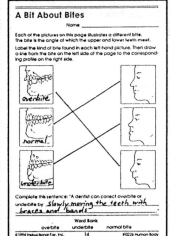

overbite

normal

underbite

Complete this sentence: "A dentist can correct overbite or underbite by _slowly moving the teeth with braces and bands_.

Four Kinds of Teeth

Name _____

You have four kinds of teeth in your mouth. Label the adult teeth pictured below.

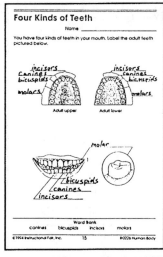

incisors
canines
bicuspids
molars

incisors
canines
bicuspids
molars

Adult upper   Adult lower

molar

bicuspids
canines
incisors

Bones (Skeletal System Review)

Name _____

Complete the puzzle.

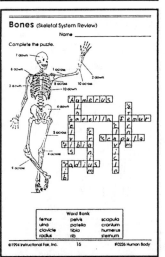

Muscle Man

Name _____

There are hundreds of muscle groups in your body. Label these muscles that appear on the surface of your body.

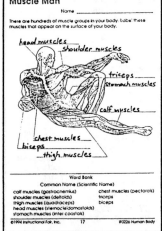

head muscles

shoulder muscles

triceps

stomach muscles

calf muscles

chest muscles

biceps

thigh muscles

Skeletal Muscles

Name _____

Skeletal muscles are attached to the skeleton by means of tendons.

Label the parts of the arm pictured below.

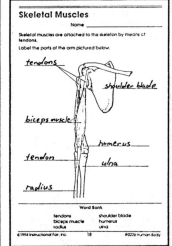

tendons

shoulder blade

biceps muscle

humerus

tendon

ulna

radius

Your Muscles

Name _____

Label the three different kinds of muscles in section A. Give an example of the work they do.

Label the muscle parts in section B.

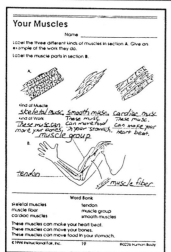

Kind of Muscle
skeletal musc. smooth musc. cardiac musc.
These musc.   These musc.   These musc.
move your bones. can move food can make your
                  in your stomach. heart beat.

muscle group

tendon

muscle fiber

Word Bank
skeletal muscles	tendon
muscle fiber	muscle group
cardiac muscles	smooth muscles

These muscles can make your heart beat.
These muscles can move your bones.
These muscles can move food in your stomach.

Working Pairs

Name _____

The muscles in both your upper arms and upper legs are very much alike. They both work in pairs to help raise and lower the limbs. Label the parts of these "working pairs."

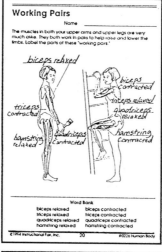

biceps relaxed

biceps contracted

triceps contracted

triceps relaxed

quadriceps relaxed

hamstring relaxed

quadriceps contracted

hamstring contracted

Word Bank
biceps relaxed	biceps contracted
triceps relaxed	triceps contracted
quadriceps relaxed	quadriceps contracted
hamstring relaxed	hamstring contracted

Your Circulatory System

Name _____

Label the parts of your circulatory system.

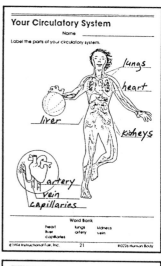

lungs

heart

liver

kidneys

artery

vein

capillaries

Word Bank
heart	lungs	kidneys
liver	artery	vein
capillaries		

Veins and Arteries

Name _____

Arteries | Veins

Draw red arrows on the arteries showing the flow of blood away from the heart.

Draw blue arrows on the veins showing the flow of blood back to the heart.

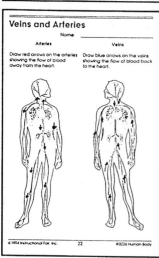

Your Heart

Name _____

Label the parts of your heart.

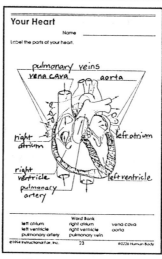

pulmonary veins

vena cava

aorta

right atrium

left atrium

right ventricle

left ventricle

pulmonary artery

Word Bank
left atrium	right atrium	vena cava
left ventricle	right ventricle	aorta
pulmonary artery	pulmonary vein	

Lub – Dub, Lub – Dub
(Circulatory System Review)

Name _____

Use the Word Bank to complete the puzzle.

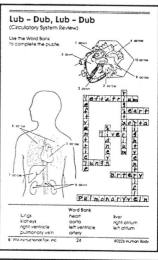

Word Bank
lungs	heart	liver
kidneys	aorta	right atrium
right ventricle	left ventricle	left atrium
pulmonary vein	artery	

Your Respiratory System

Name _____

Label the parts of your respiratory system.

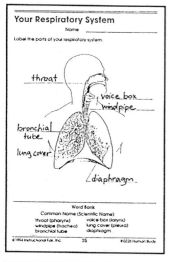

throat

voice box

windpipe

bronchial tube

lung cover

diaphragm

Word Bank
Common Name (Scientific Name)	
throat (pharynx)	voice box (larynx)
windpipe (trachea)	lung cover (pleura)
bronchial tube	diaphragm

Your Lungs

Name _____

Label the parts of your lungs.

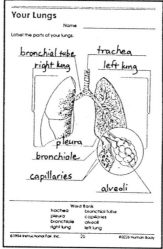

bronchial tube

trachea

right lung

left lung

pleura

bronchiole

capillaries

alveoli

Word Bank
trachea	bronchial tube
pleura	capillaries
bronchiole	alveoli
right lung	left lung

Breathe In! Breathe Out!

Name _____

You breathe in and breathe out almost 20,000 times each day! Label these two pictures either Inhale (breathe in) or Exhale (breathe out). Label the other parts of your breathing system using the Word Bank.

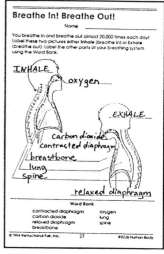

INHALE

oxygen

EXHALE

carbon dioxide

contracted diaphragm

breastbone

lung

spine

relaxed diaphragm

Word Bank
contracted diaphragm	oxygen
carbon dioxide	lung
relaxed diaphragm	spine
breastbone	

Huff – Puff (Respiratory System Review)

Use the Word Bank to complete the puzzle.

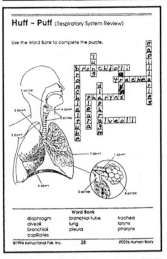

Word Bank

diaphragm	bronchial tube	trachea
alveoli	lung	larynx
bronchioi	pleura	pharynx
capillaries		

©1994 Instructional Fair, Inc.   28   IF0226 Human Body

Your Digestive System

Name

Label the parts of your digestive system.

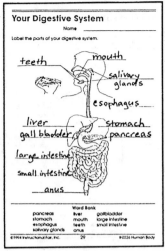

Word Bank

pancreas	liver	gallbladder
stomach	mouth	large intestine
esophagus	teeth	small intestine
salivary glands	anus	

©1994 Instructional Fair, Inc.   29   IF0226 Human Body

The Alimentary Canal

Name

The main part of the digestive system is the alimentary canal, a tube which starts at the mouth, and travels through the body ending at the anus.
Label the parts of the alimentary canal.

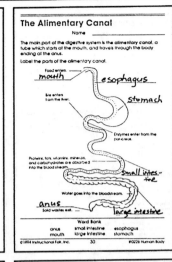

Word Bank

anus	small intestine	esophagus
mouth	large intestine	stomach

©1994 Instructional Fair, Inc.   30   IF0226 Human Body

The Stomach

The stomach is the widest part of the alimentary canal. The stomach has three layers of muscles which allow it to contract in different directions. The contracting motion mashes food and mixes it with digestive juices.
Label the parts of the stomach and the tubes leading into and out of the esophagus.

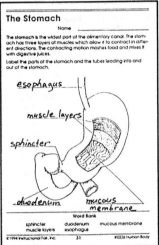

Word Bank

sphincter	duodenum	mucous membrane
muscle layers	esophagus	

©1994 Instructional Fair, Inc.   31   IF0226 Human Body

Digestion in the Mouth

Name

Label the parts of the digestive system located in and around the mouth.

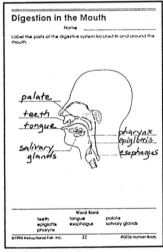

Word Bank

teeth	tongue	palate
epiglottis	esophagus	salivary glands
pharynx		

©1994 Instructional Fair, Inc.   32   IF0226 Human Body

Digestion Helpers

Name

Label these organs that aid in the digestion of the food you eat.

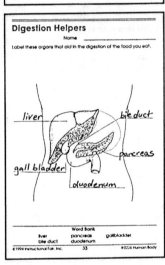

Word Bank

liver	pancreas	gallbladder
bile duct	duodenum	

©1994 Instructional Fair, Inc.   33   IF0226 Human Body

Gulp, Gulp (Digestive System Review)

Use the Word Bank to complete the puzzle.

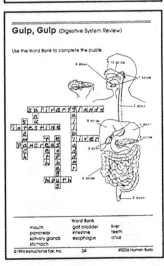

Word Bank

mouth	gall bladder	liver
pancreas	intestine	teeth
salivary glands	esophagus	anus

©1994 Instructional Fair, Inc.   34   IF0226 Human Body

Let's Look in Your Mouth!

Name

What do you see when you open your mouth in front of a mirror? Label the different parts.

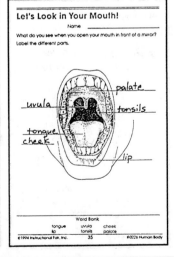

Word Bank

tongue	uvula	cheek
lip	tonsils	palate

©1994 Instructional Fair, Inc.   35   IF0226 Human Body

Blood Scrubbers

Name

Label the different parts of your body's urinary system.

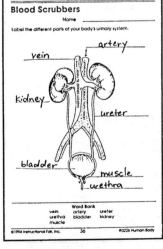

Word Bank

vein	artery	ureter
urethra	bladder	kidney
muscle		

©1994 Instructional Fair, Inc.   36   IF0226 Human Body

Your Central Nervous System

Name _____

Label the parts of your central nervous system.

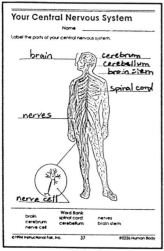

brain
cerebrum
cerebellum
brain stem
spinal cord
nerves
nerve cell

Word Bank

brain	spinal cord	nerves
cerebrum	cerebellum	brain stem
nerve cell		

Neurons

Name _____

Label the parts of a neuron.

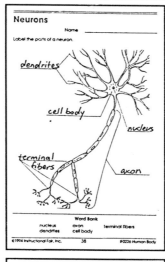

dendrites
cell body
nucleus
terminal fibers
axon

Word Bank

nucleus	axon	terminal fibers
dendrites	cell body	

Transmitters of Impulses

Name _____

Neurons act as "go betweens" in the sending and receiving of impulses within the nervous system. The drawings below illustrate how impulses pass from one neuron to another.

Label the parts of the enlarged illustration.

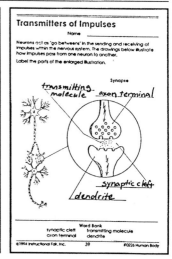

Synapse
transmitting molecule
axon terminal
synaptic cleft
dendrite

Word Bank

synaptic cleft	transmitting molecule
axon terminal	dendrite

Exploring Your Brain

Name _____

Label the parts of your brain.

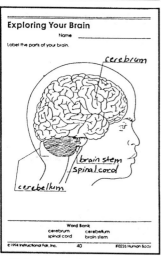

cerebrum
brain stem
spinal cord
cerebellum

Word Bank

cerebrum	cerebellum
spinal cord	brain stem

Nervous System

Name _____

Two of the nervous systems in the human body are the central and the peripheral.

Label these two systems and their parts.

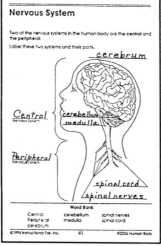

cerebrum
Central Nervous System
cerebellum
medulla
Peripheral Nervous System
spinal cord
spinal nerves

Word Bank

Central	cerebellum	spinal nerves
Peripheral	medulla	spinal cord
cerebrum		

Control Central (Nervous System Review)

Name _____

Use the Word Bank to complete the puzzle.

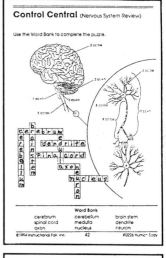

cerebrum
dendrite
spinal cord
axon
nucleus
cerebellum

Word Bank

cerebrum	cerebellum	brain stem
spinal cord	medulla	dendrite
axon	nucleus	neuron

Autonomic Nervous System

Name _____

The autonomic nervous system works almost independently of the central nervous system. It controls the life-sustaining functions of the body, such as breathing, digestion and heartbeat. These organs and muscle tissue work involuntarily.

Label these important parts.

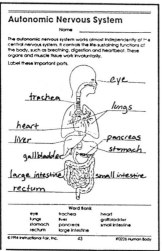

eye
trachea
lungs
heart
liver
pancreas
stomach
gallbladder
large intestine
small intestine
rectum

Word Bank

eye	trachea	heart
lungs	liver	gallbladder
stomach	pancreas	small intestine
rectum	large intestine	

Your Endocrine System

Name _____

The endocrine glands help control many of your body's functions.

Label the glands of the Endocrine System.

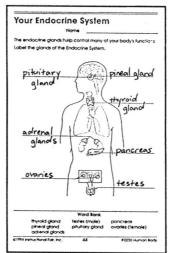

pituitary gland
pineal gland
thyroid gland
adrenal glands
pancreas
ovaries
testes

Word Bank

thyroid gland	testes (male)	pancreas
pineal gland	pituitary gland	ovaries (female)
adrenal glands		

Glands at Work

Name _____

Draw a line from the name of the gland to its picture.
Draw a line from the picture of the gland to its function.

Gland

thyroid
pituitary
parathyroids
adrenal
thymus
ovaries
pancreas

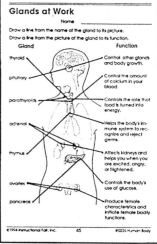

Function

- Control other glands and body growth.
- Control the amount of calcium in your blood.
- Controls the rate that food is turned into energy.
- Helps the body's immune system to recognize and reject germs.
- Affects kidneys and helps you when you are excited, angry, or frightened.
- Controls the body's use of glucose.
- Produce female characteristics and initiate female bodily functions.

Your Sensory Systems

Name _____

Your brain gets information from outside your body through many different sense organs. Label the different sense organs and the nerve cells pictured on this page.

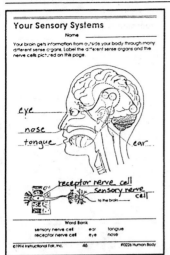

eye
nose
tongue
ear

receptor nerve cell
sensory nerve cell
to the brain

It Tastes Great!

Name _____

Your tongue can sense four basic tastes – sweet, sour, bitter and salty. Label the different areas of the tongue and the different parts of this sense organ.

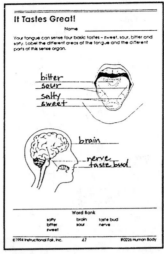

bitter
sour
salty
sweet

brain

nerve
taste bud

Your Nose

Name _____

Label the parts of your nose.

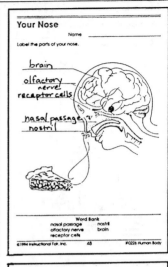

brain
olfactory
nerve
receptor cells

nasal passage
nostril

Your Ear

Name _____

Label the parts of your ear.

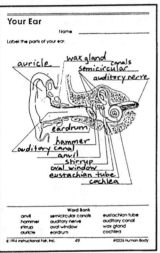

auricle
wax gland
semicircular   canals
auditory nerve

eardrum
hammer
auditory canal
anvil
stirrup
oval window
eustachian tube
cochlea

Ear, Nose and Throat Connection

Name _____

Your ears, nose, mouth and throat are all connected to each other. Label the parts in the picture below.

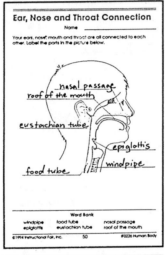

nasal passage
roof of the mouth

eustachian tube

epiglottis

food tube   windpipe

Inside Your Eye

Name _____

Label the parts of your eye pictured below.

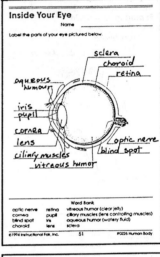

sclera
choroid
retina

aqueous
humour

iris
pupil

cornea
lens
ciliary muscles
vitreous humor

optic nerve
blind spot

Eyes to Brain Connection

Name _____

Your eyes gather the rays of light coming off an object. They change the light rays into nerve impulses, but your brain interprets these impulses and "draws" a picture of the image. Label the parts of this eye to brain connection.

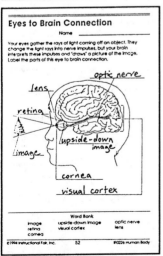

optic nerve
lens
retina
upside-down
image
image
cornea
visual cortex

Eye Protection

Name _____

Your eyeball is very well protected. Label the parts of the eye and nose that help protect it.

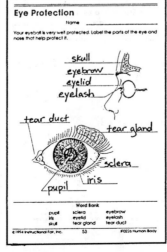

skull
eyebrow
eyelid
eyelash

tear duct
tear gland

sclera
iris
pupil

Your Eye - The Camera

Name _____

Your eye is very similar to a camera. Label the parts of the eye and the camera. Also, give the job of each part.

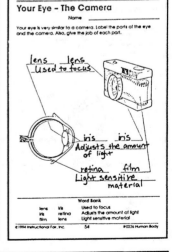

lens   lens
Used to focus

iris   iris
Adjusts the amount
of light

retina   film
Light sensitive
material

Your Eyesight

Name _____

Eyes can vary in shape. This can give people problems with their sight. Label the eyes below.

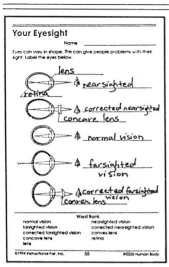

lens
retina
→ nearsighted

→ corrected nearsighted
concave lens

→ normal vision

→ farsighted vision

→ corrected farsighted vision
convex lens

Word Bank

normal vision · nearsighted vision
farsighted vision · corrected nearsighted vision
corrected farsighted vision · convex lens
concave lens · retina
lens

©1994 Instructional Fair, Inc.   55   IF0226 Human Body

Sensational! (Ear and Eye Review)

Name _____

Use the Word Bank to complete the puzzle.

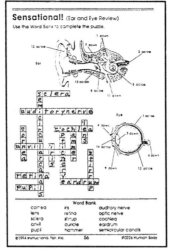

Word Bank

cornea · iris · auditory nerve
lens · retina · optic nerve
sclera · stirrup · cochlea
anvil · auricle · eardrum
pupil · hammer · semicircular canals

©1994 Instructional Fair, Inc.   56   IF0226 Human Body

Skin Deep

Name _____

Your skin is made up of many layers. These layers contain hairs, nerves, blood vessels and glands. Label these layers and parts.

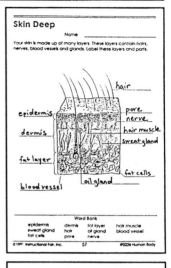

hair
epidermis
pore
nerve
dermis
hair muscle
sweat gland
fat layer
fat cells
blood vessel
oil gland

Word Bank

epidermis · dermis · fat layer · hair muscle
sweat gland · hair · oil gland · blood vessel
fat cells · pore · nerve

©1994 Instructional Fair, Inc.   57   IF0226 Human Body

Sweaty Palms and Goose Bumps

Name _____

Your body has its own air conditioning system. On cold days your skin has a way to keep in your body's warmth. On hot days your skin can cool you off.

Label the two pictures either Warm Day or Cool Day. Label the parts of the skin using the Word Bank.

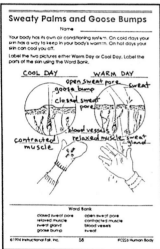

COOL DAY
WARM DAY
open sweat pore
goose bump
sweat
closed sweat pore
blood vessels
contracted muscle
relaxed muscle
sweat gland

Word Bank

closed sweat pore · open sweat pore
relaxed muscle · contracted muscle
sweat gland · blood vessels
goose bump · sweat

©1994 Instructional Fair, Inc.   58   IF0226 Human Body

Fingerprints

Name _____

The ridges in fingertips form unique patterns. No two people have the same pattern, not even identical twins. The ridges on fingers form three main groups of patterns – the arch, the loop, and the whorl.

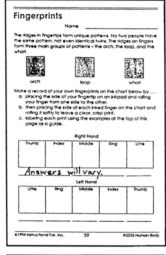

arch   loop   whorl

Make a record of your own fingerprints on the chart below by . . .
a. placing the side of your fingertip on an inkpad and rolling your finger from one side to the other.
b. then placing the side of each inked finger on the chart and rolling it softly to leave a clear, crisp print.
c. labeling each print using the examples at the top of this page as a guide.

Right Hand

Thumb	Index	Middle	Ring	Little

Answers will vary.

Left Hand

Little	Ring	Middle	Index	Thumb

©1994 Instructional Fair, Inc.   59   IF0226 Human Body

Your Toenails and Fingernails

Name _____

Nails are a specialized part of your skin that protect the ends of your toes and fingers. Label the parts of the nails below.

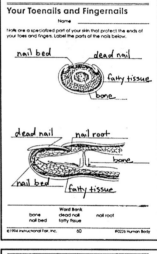

nail bed
dead nail
fatty tissue
bone

dead nail
nail root
bone
nail bed
fatty tissue

Word Bank

bone · dead nail · nail root
nail bed · fatty tissue

©1994 Instructional Fair, Inc.   60   IF0226 Human Body

Reproductive System – Male

Name _____

The purpose of the reproductive system is to create new life. Label the parts of the male reproductive system.

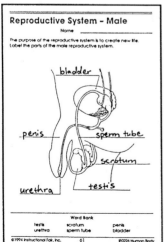

bladder
penis
sperm tube
scrotum
urethra
testis

Word Bank

testis · scrotum · penis
urethra · sperm tube · bladder

©1994 Instructional Fair, Inc.   61   IF0226 Human Body

Reproductive System – Female

Name _____

The purpose of the reproductive system is to create new life. Label the parts of the female reproductive system.

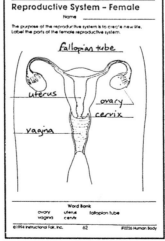

fallopian tube
uterus
ovary
cervix
vagina

Word Bank

ovary · uterus · fallopian tube
vagina · cervix

©1994 Instructional Fair, Inc.   62   IF0226 Human Body

New Life

Name _____

From the time of conception, a single cell divides and keeps on dividing until it forms the six trillion cells of a human newborn baby. This development takes nine months.

Beneath each picture write the matching description.

4 weeks
Develops arm and leg buds; heart begins to beat.

5 weeks
Ears, eyes, nose, fingers and toes are formed.

3 months
Has recognizable human features; sex can be determined.

14 months
First movements felt; heartbeat can be heard with a stethoscope.

7 months
Can survive birth with special care.

9 months
Fully developed with organs that can function on their own.

Word Bank

• Fully developed with organs that can function on their own.
• Develops tiny arm and leg buds, and its heart begins to beat.
• Ears, nose, fingers, and toes are formed.
• Can survive birth with special care.
• First movements felt and heartbeat can be heard with a stethoscope.
• Has recognizable human features and sex can be determined.

©1994 Instructional Fair, Inc.   63   IF0226 Human Body

    IF0226 Human Body

Birth of a Baby

When a baby is fully developed within the uterus, a hormone in the pituitary gland stimulates the muscles of the uterus. These muscle contractions signal the beginning of labor. The opening to the uterus, the cervix, gradually enlarges to allow the baby to pass through. The amniotic sac that surrounds the baby will break, releasing a gush of amniotic fluid. After the baby is born, the placenta separates from the wall of the uterus and is pushed out by more muscle contractions.

Study and label the diagram of the birth of a baby.

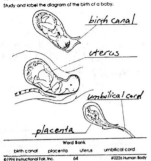

birth canal
uterus
umbilical cord
placenta

Word Bank

birth canal   placenta   uterus   umbilical cord

©1994 Instructional Fair, Inc.   64   IF0226 Human Body

Organ Systems

Make an X in the correct box to show to which system/systems each organ belongs. One is done for you.

Organs	Diges-tive	Respi-ratory	Urinary	Repro-ductive	Circula-tory	Ner-vous	Endo-crine
Bladder			X				
Brain						X	
Heart					X		
Ovaries				X			
Liver	X						
Pancreas	X						
Kidneys			X				
Spinal Cord						X	
Lungs		X					
Small intestines	X						
Diaphragm		X					
Mouth	X	X					
Nerves						X	
Testes				X			X
Thyroid Gland							X
Arteries		X			X		
Esophagus	X						
Cerebellum						X	

©1994 Instructional Fair, Inc.   65   IF0226 Human Body

Feel the Beat

When the heart pumps, it forces blood out into the arteries. The walls of the arteries expand and contract to the rhythm of the heart which creates a pulse.

You can feel your pulse where the arteries are close to the surface of the skin. Two good places to feel a pulse are on the inside of the wrist, and on the neck to the side of the windpipe.

Try the experiments below and complete the chart by . . .

1. counting the number of heart beats in 15 seconds.
2. multiplying that number by 4 to get the pulse rate for one minute.

Study your results. Explain how each activity affected your pulse rate.

Answers will vary.

Activity	Pulse Rate for 15 sec.	X 4 =	Pulse Rate per minute
Sitting still for 10 minutes			
Running in place for 3 minutes.			
Just after finishing your lunch or dinner.			
While still in bed in the morning.			
Just after getting ready for school.			

©1994 Instructional Fair, Inc.   66   IF0226 Human Body

Pressure Points

When a person is severely cut and begins to bleed, it's time for quick action. First aid for severe bleeding involves applying pressure over the wound. Sometimes it is possible to press the artery above the wound against the bone behind it, and stop the bleeding. This place is called a pressure point. A pressure point is also an excellent location to take a person's pulse.

Place an X on the pressure points listed in the Word Bank.

Word Bank

neck   behind the knee   inside the thigh
wrist   bend of elbow   top of foot

©1994 Instructional Fair, Inc.   67   IF0226 Human Body

Name the Nutrient

Your body is made up of millions of cells that need food to stay alive. Your body needs nutrients from the foods you eat to help the cells grow and repair themselves. Nutrients are divided into six major groups: fats, proteins, carbohydrates, minerals, vitamins and water.

Read each clue. Identify these five nutrients.

"I'm the body's building material. You need me to make new tissue. You get plenty of me from milk, beans, meat, and peanuts."

Who am I?   __protein__

"I give you energy to work and play. You can find me in starchy foods like pasta and potatoes."

Who am I?   __carbohydrate__

"I help build strong bones and teeth. I also give you healthy red blood. You can find me in all four food groups."

Who am I?   __mineral__

"I give you a concentrated source of energy. You can find me in oily and greasy foods, like bacon, salad dressing, and butter. I also help you maintain healthy skin and hair."

Who am I?   __fat__

"You might call me the alphabet soup of the nutrients. I am one of the essential nutrients. I don't give you energy, but I do help your body get energy from the other nutrients."

Who am I?   __vitamin__

Word Bank

fat
protein
carbohydrate
vitamin
mineral

©1994 Instructional Fair, Inc.   68   IF0226 Human Body

You Are What You Eat

Looking closely at the information on a cereal box you can learn many interesting things about the product.

Carefully read the information on this example from a cereal box. Answer the questions. Compare these answers with the information found on a box of cereal you might eat for breakfast.

	Corn Balls	Your Cereal
What kind of grain(s) is used?	corn	Answers will vary
Is sugar used?	yes	
What position is sugar on the list of ingredients?	2nd	
List other sweeteners	corn syrup and molasses	
How many calories per serving without milk.	110	
How many calories per serving when eaten with 1/2 cup of skim milk?	150	
How much protein per serving?	1g	
How many vitamins and minerals does the cereal contain?	10	
How much cholesterol is in one serving?	0 mg	

©1994 Instructional Fair, Inc.   69   IF0226 Human Body

Reading the Label

The labels on medicine containers give us important information. Labels should always be read carefully.

Read the information on the cough medicine labels below. Answer the questions.

Recommended Dosage:
Children (6 - 12 years): 1 teaspoon every 6 hours.
Adult: 2 teaspoons every 6 hours.
Caution: Do not administer to children under 5. No more than 4 dosages per day. This product may cause drowsiness; use caution if operating machinery or driving a vehicle. Should not be taken if you are pregnant or nursing a child.
If cough or fever persists, consult a physician.
Exp. Date: 8/94

1. What is the adult dosage?   __2 tsp every 6 hours__
2. What is a child's dosage?   __1 tsp. every 6 hours__
3. What is a side effect of this medicine?   __drowsiness__
4. Who should not take this medicine?   __child under 5;__   __pregnant or nursing mother__
5. How many dosages per day can be taken safely?   __4__
6. What is the expiration date of this medicine?   __Aug., 1994__
7. What action should be taken if the medicine does not relieve your cough?   __Consult your physician__
8. For what symptoms should this medicine be taken?   __Coughs due to colds and flu.__

©1994 Instructional Fair, Inc.   70   IF0226 Human Body

Caution: Poison!

Children are always very curious. They love to touch things and pick them up. Very young children like to put things into their mouths. What action do you take if a child swallows a poisonous material?

CALL YOUR POISON CONTROL CENTER, HOSPITAL, PHYSICIAN, OR EMERGENCY PHONE NUMBER IMMEDIATELY!

If you cannot obtain emergency advice, follow these procedures.

- If the poison is corrosive: paint remover, household cleaners, gasoline, drain cleaner, ammonia or lye, DO NOT make the patient vomit. Give the patient water or milk to dilute the poison.
- If the poison is not corrosive: insect spray, aspirin, pesticides or medicine, make the patient vomit, or use a poison control kit. To force the patient to vomit touch the back of his/her throat.

Write a bold "V" on each picture that shows poison that should be vomited if swallowed. Circle each poison that should not be vomited if swallowed.

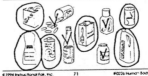

©1994 Instructional Fair, Inc.   71   IF0226 Human Body

Human Body Review

Use the Word Bank to complete the puzzle.

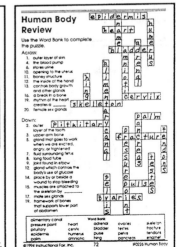

Across:
1. outer layer of skin
4. the blood pump
6. stores urine
10. opening to the uterus
11. boney structure
12. the inside of the hand
13. controls body growth and other glands
16. a break in a bone
19. rhythm of the heart creates a _____
20. female sex glands

Down:
2. outer
5. structure of the tooth
7. upper arm bone
8. gland that goes to work when we are excited, angry, or frightened
9. fluid surrounding fetus
13. long food tube
14. joint found in elbow
15. gland which controls the body's use of glucose
14. place by or beside a wound to stop bleeding
15. muscles are attached to the skeleton by
17. male sex glands
18. framework of bones that supports lower part of abdomen

Word Bank

alimentary canal   heart   ovaries   skeleton
pressure point   cervix   bladder   fracture
pituitary   humerus   pulse   pelvis
epidermis   amniotic   king   pancreas
palm   enamel

©1994 Instructional Fair, Inc.   72   IF0226 Human Body

©1994 Instructional Fair, Inc.   IF0226 Human Body

Your Nervous System

Label the parts of your nervous system.

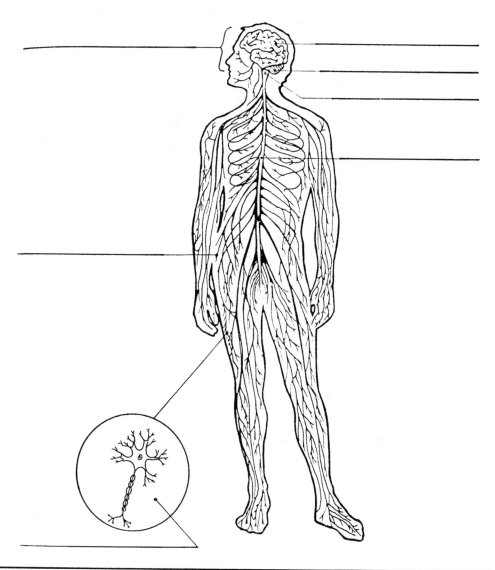

Word Bank

brain   spinal cord   nerves
cerebrum   cerebellum   brain stem
nerve cell

©1994 Instructional Fair, Inc.   37   IF0226 Human Body

Neurons

Label the parts of a neuron.

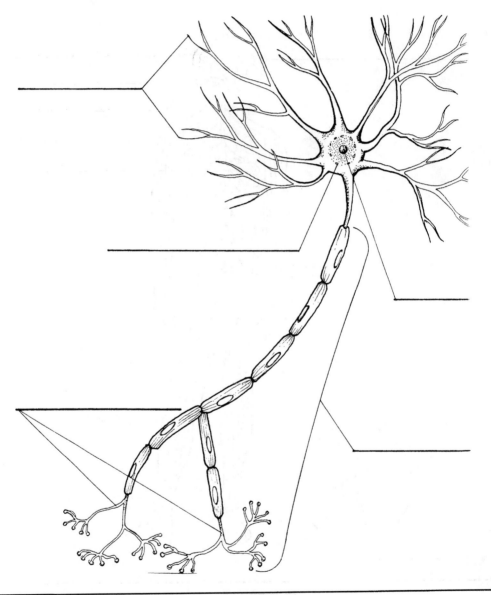

Transmitters of Impulses

Neurons act as "go betweens" in the sending and receiving of impulses within the nervous system. The drawings below illustrate how impulses pass from one neuron to another.

Label the parts of the enlarged illustration.

Synapse

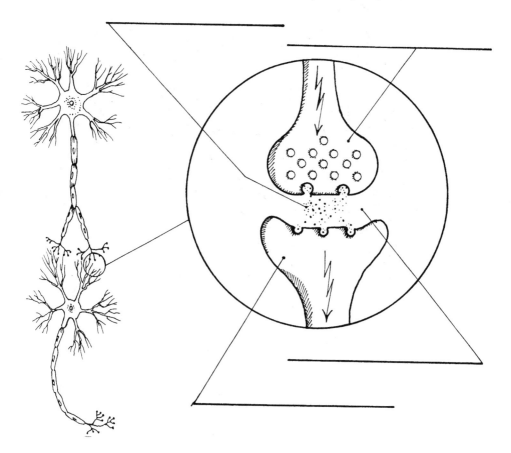

Exploring Your Brain

Label the parts of your brain.

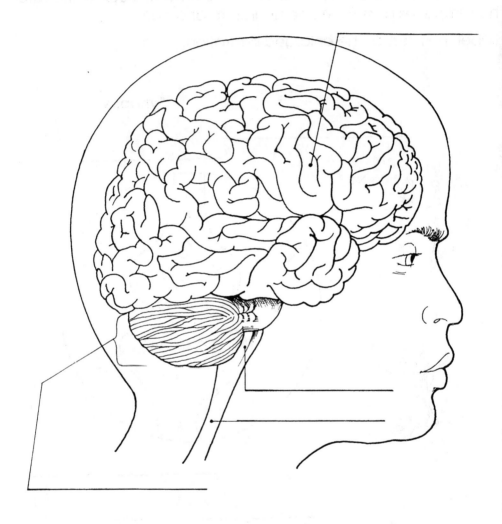

Nervous System

Two of the nervous systems in the human body are the **central** and the **peripheral**.

Label these two systems and their parts.

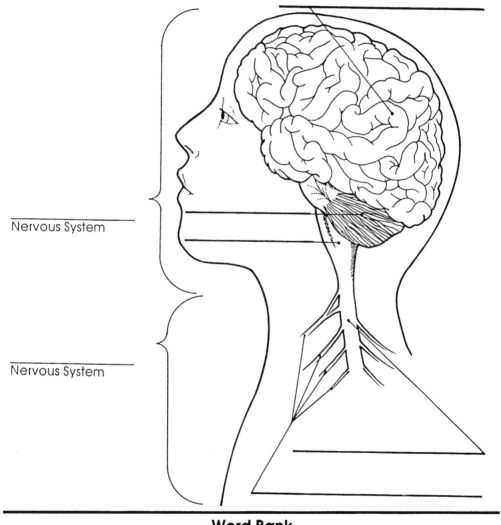

Nervous System

Nervous System

Word Bank

Central	cerebellum	spinal nerves
Peripheral	medulla	spinal cord
cerebrum		

Control Central (Nervous System Review)

Use the Word Bank to complete the puzzle.

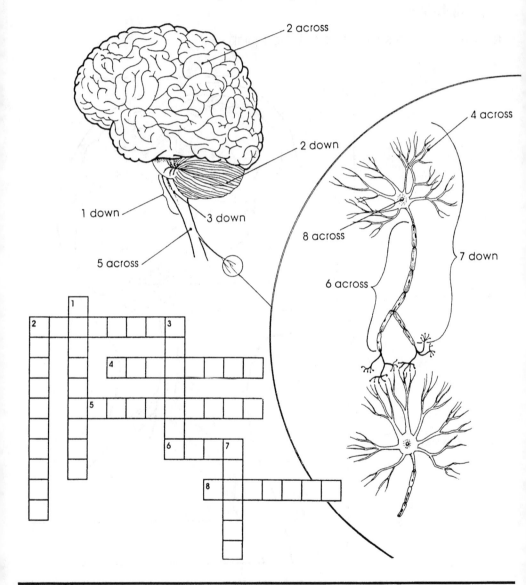

Word Bank

cerebrum	cerebellum	brain stem
spinal cord	medulla	dendrite
axon	nucleus	neuron

42

Autonomic Nervous System

The **autonomic nervous system** works almost independently of the central nervous system. It controls the life-sustaining functions of the body, such as breathing, digestion and heartbeat. These organs and muscle tissue work involuntarily.

Label these important parts.

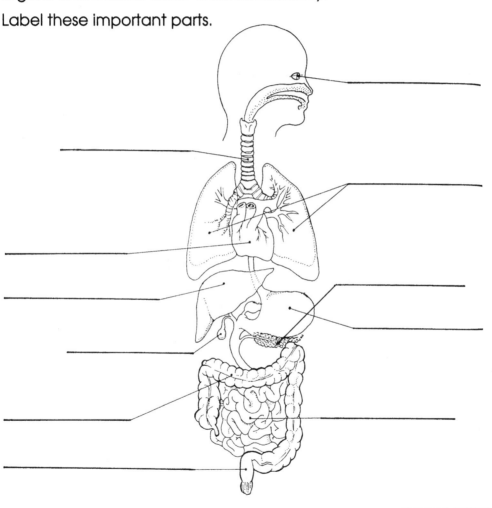

Word Bank

eye	trachea	heart
lungs	liver	gallbladder
stomach	pancreas	small intestine
rectum	large intestine	

Your Endocrine System

The endocrine glands help control many of your body's functions.
Label the glands of the endocrine system.

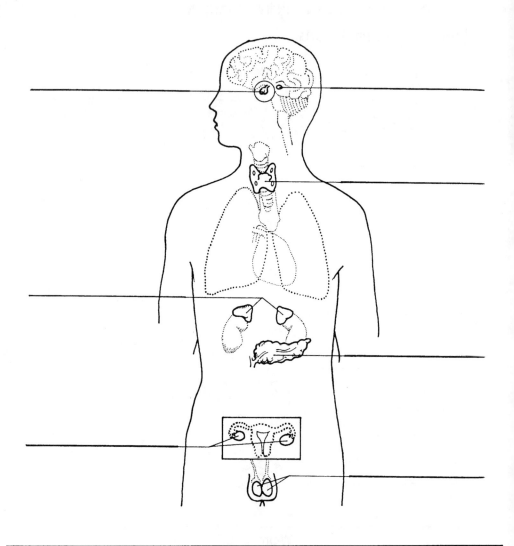

Word Bank

thyroid gland	testes (male)	pancreas
pineal gland	pituitary gland	ovaries (female)
adrenal glands		

Glands at Work

Draw a line from the name of the gland to its picture.

Draw a line from the picture of the gland to its function.

Gland		Function

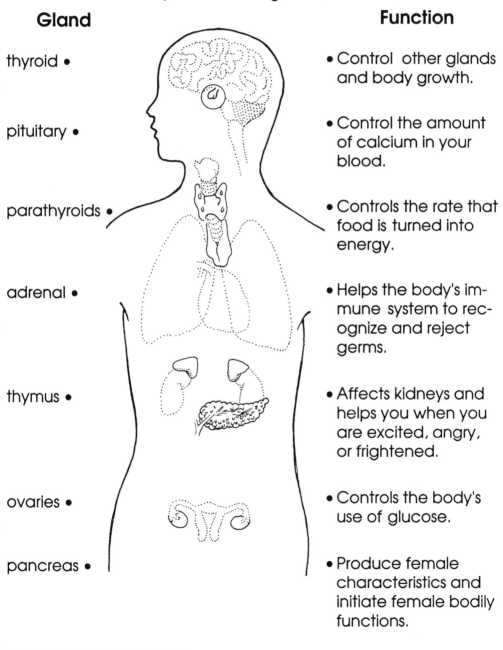

thyroid •

pituitary •

parathyroids •

adrenal •

thymus •

ovaries •

pancreas •

• Control other glands and body growth.

• Control the amount of calcium in your blood.

• Controls the rate that food is turned into energy.

• Helps the body's immune system to recognize and reject germs.

• Affects kidneys and helps you when you are excited, angry, or frightened.

• Controls the body's use of glucose.

• Produce female characteristics and initiate female bodily functions.

Your Sensory Systems

Your brain gets information from outside your body through many different sense organs. Label the different sense organs and the nerve cells pictured on this page.

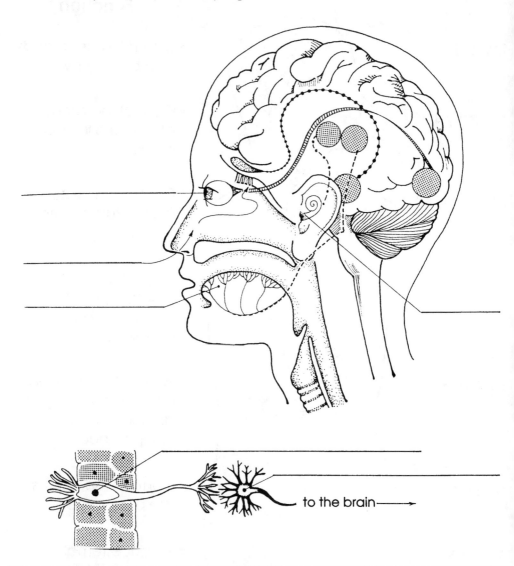

to the brain⟶

Word Bank

sensory nerve cell	ear	tongue
receptor nerve cell	eye	nose

It Tastes Great!

Your tongue can sense four basic tastes – sweet, sour, bitter and salty. Label the different areas of the tongue and the different parts of this sense organ.

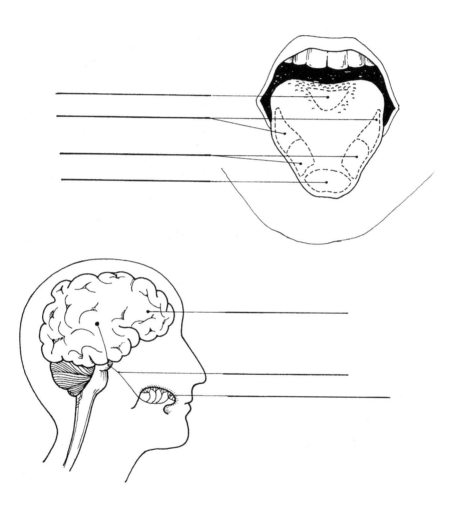

Word Bank

salty	brain	taste bud
bitter	sour	nerve
sweet		

Your Nose

Label the parts of your nose.

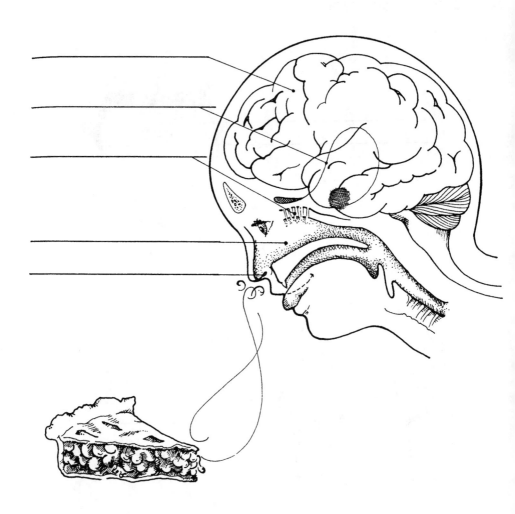

Word Bank

nasal passage   nostril

olfactory nerve   brain

receptor cells

Your Ear

Label the parts of your ear.

Word Bank

anvil	semicircular canals	eustachian tube
hammer	auditory nerve	auditory canal
stirrup	oval window	wax gland
auricle	eardrum	cochlea

Ear, Nose and Throat Connection

Your ears, nose, mouth and throat are all connected to each other. Label the parts in the picture below.

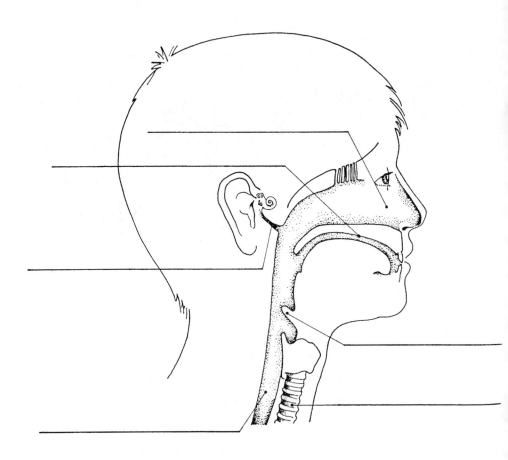

Word Bank

windpipe	food tube	nasal passage
epiglottis	eustachian tube	roof of the mouth

Inside Your Eye

Label the parts of your eye pictured below.

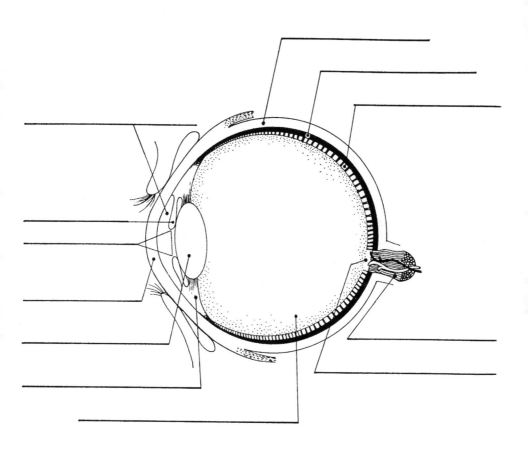

Word Bank

optic nerve	retina	vitreous humor (clear jelly)
cornea	pupil	ciliary muscles (lens controlling muscles)
blind spot	iris	aqueous humor (watery fluid)
choroid	lens	sclera

Eyes-to-Brain Connection

Your eyes gather the rays of light coming off an object. They change the light rays into nerve impulses, but your brain interprets these impulses and "draws" a picture of the image. Label the parts of this eye-to-brain connection.

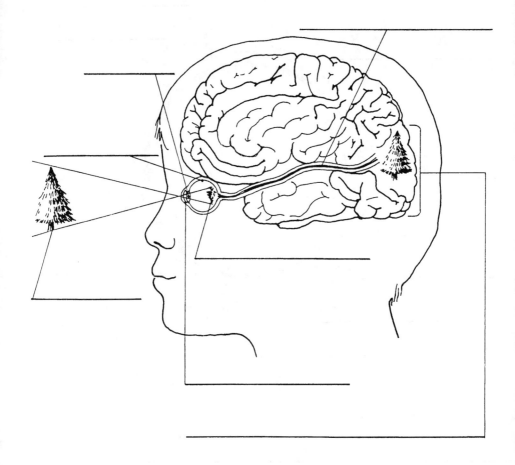

Word Bank

image   upside-down image   optic nerve
retina   visual cortex   lens
cornea

Eye Protection

Your eyeball is very well protected. Label the parts of the eye and nose that help protect it.

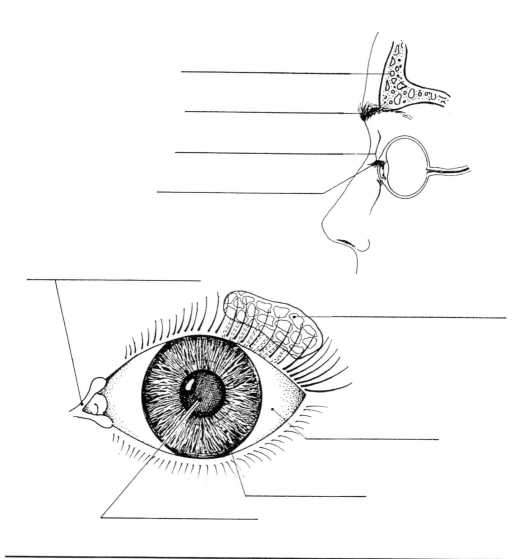

Word Bank

pupil	sclera	eyebrow
iris	eyelid	eyelash
skull	tear gland	tear duct

Your Eye - The Camera

Your eye is very similar to a camera. Label the parts of the eye and the camera. Also, give the job of each part.

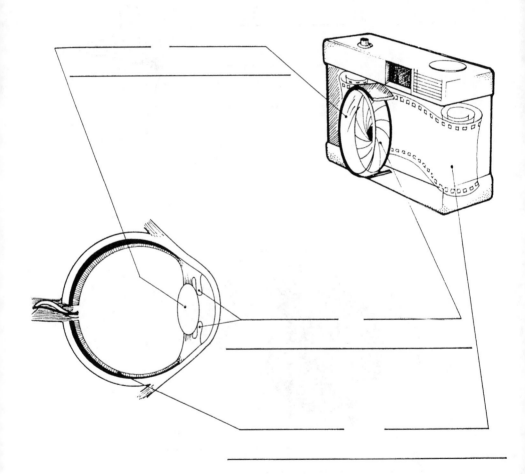

Word Bank

lens	iris	Used to focus
iris	retina	Adjusts the amount of light
film	lens	Light sensitive material

Your Eyesight

Eyes can vary in shape. This can give people problems with their sight. Label the eyes below.

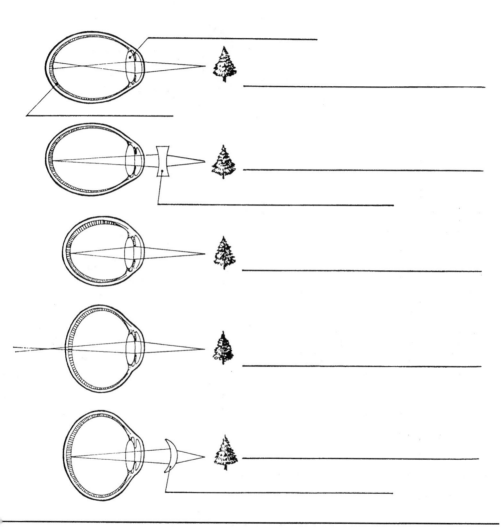

Word Bank

normal vision

nearsighted vision

farsighted vision

corrected nearsighted vision

corrected farsighted vision

convex lens

concave lens

retina

lens

 IF0226 Human Body

Sensational! (Ear and Eye Review)

Use the Word Bank to complete the puzzle.

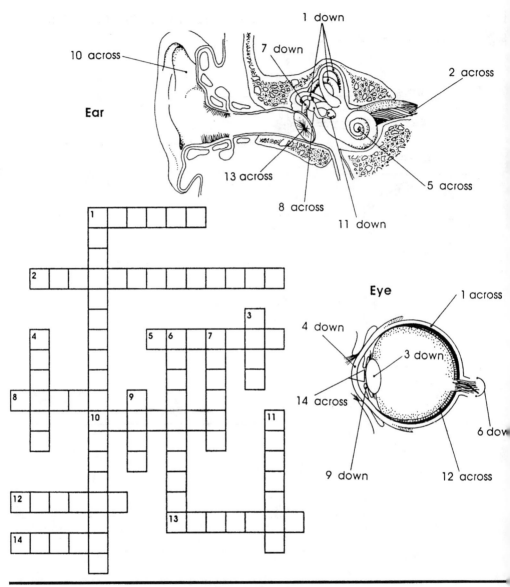

Ear

1 down
7 down
10 across
2 across
13 across
8 across
11 down
5 across

Eye

1 across
4 down
3 down
14 across
6 down
9 down
12 across

Word Bank

cornea	iris	auditory nerve
lens	retina	optic nerve
sclera	stirrup	cochlea
anvil	auricle	eardrum
pupil	hammer	semicircular canals

Skin Deep

Your skin is made up of many layers. These layers contain hairs, nerves, blood vessels and glands. Label these layers and parts.

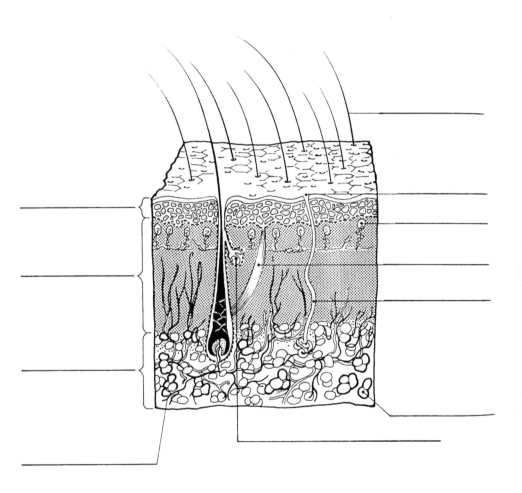

Word Bank

epidermis	dermis	fat layer	hair muscle
sweat gland	hair	oil gland	blood vessel
fat cells	pore	nerve	

Sweaty Palms and Goose Bumps

Your body has its own air conditioning system. On cold days your skin has a way to keep in your body's warmth. On hot days your skin can cool you off.

Label the two pictures either **Warm Day** or **Cool Day**. Label the parts of the skin using the Word Bank.

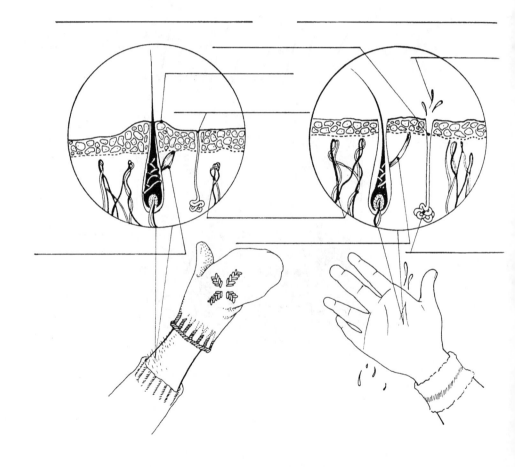

Word Bank

closed sweat pore	open sweat pore
relaxed muscle	contracted muscle
sweat gland	blood vessels
goose bump	sweat

Fingerprints

The ridges in fingertips form unique patterns. No two people have the same pattern, not even identical twins. The ridges on fingers form three main groups of patterns – the arch, the loop, and the whorl.

arch

loop

whorl

Make a record of your own fingerprints on the chart below by . . .
   a. placing the side of your fingertip on an inkpad and rolling your finger from one side to the other.
   b. then placing the side of each inked finger on the chart and rolling it softly to leave a clear, crisp print.
   c. labeling each print using the examples at the top of this page as a guide.

Right Hand

Thumb	Index	Middle	Ring	Little

Left Hand

Little	Ring	Middle	Index	Thumb

Your Toenails and Fingernails

Nails are a specialized part of your skin that protect the ends of your toes and fingers. Label the parts of the nails below.

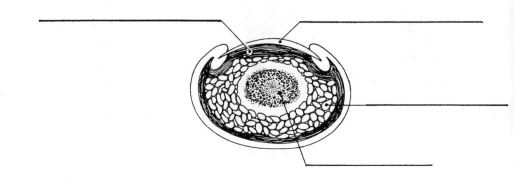

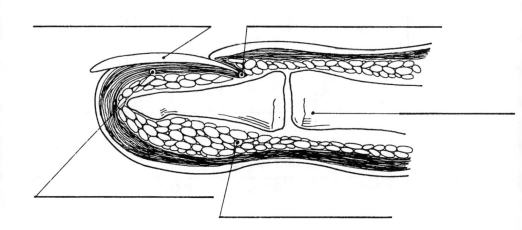

Word Bank

bone   dead nail   nail root
nail bed   fatty tissue

Reproductive System - Male

The purpose of the reproductive system is to create new life. Label the parts of the male reproductive system.

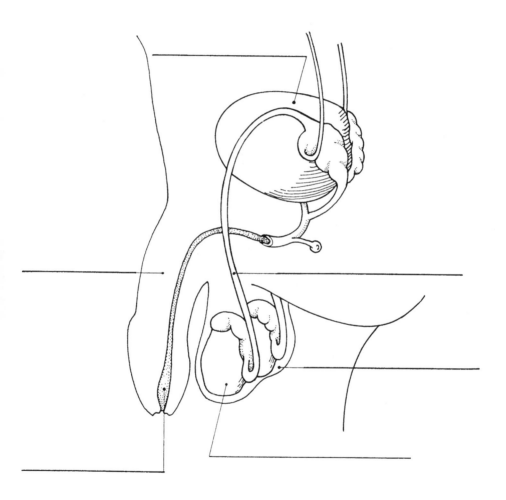

Word Bank

testis	scrotum	penis
urethra	sperm tube	bladder

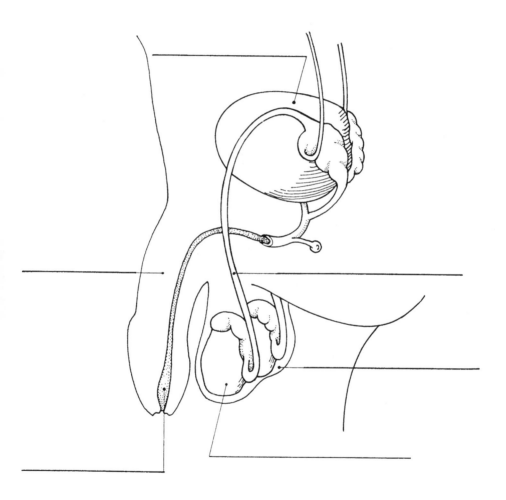

Reproductive System – Female

The purpose of the reproductive system is to create new life. Label the parts of the female reproductive system.

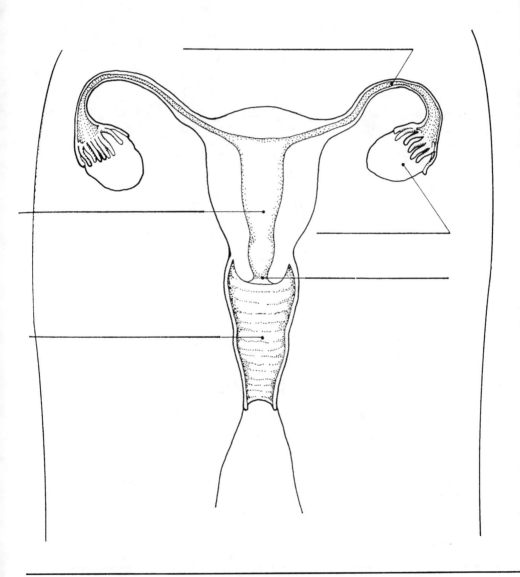

New Life

From the time of conception, a single cell divides and keeps on dividing until it forms the six trillion cells of a human newborn baby. This development takes nine months.

Beneath each picture write the matching description.

4 weeks

_____

_____

8 weeks

_____

_____

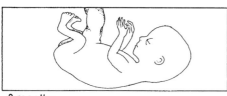

3 months

_____

_____

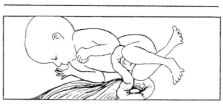

4-6 months

_____

_____

7 months

_____

_____

9 months

_____

_____

Word Bank

- Fully developed with organs that can function on their own.
- Develops tiny arm and leg buds, and its heart begins to beat.
- Ears, eyes, nose, fingers, and toes are formed.
- Can survive birth with special care.
- First movements felt and heartbeat can be heard with a stethoscope.
- Has recognizable human features and sex can be determined.

Birth of a Baby

When a baby is fully developed within the uterus, a hormone in the pituitary gland stimulates the muscles of the uterus. These muscle contractions signal the beginning of labor. The opening to the uterus, the cervix, gradually enlarges to allow the baby to pass through. The amniotic sac that surrounds the baby will break, releasing a gush of amniotic fluid. After the baby is born, the placenta separates from the wall of the uterus and is pushed out by more muscle contractions.

Study and label the diagram of the birth of a baby.

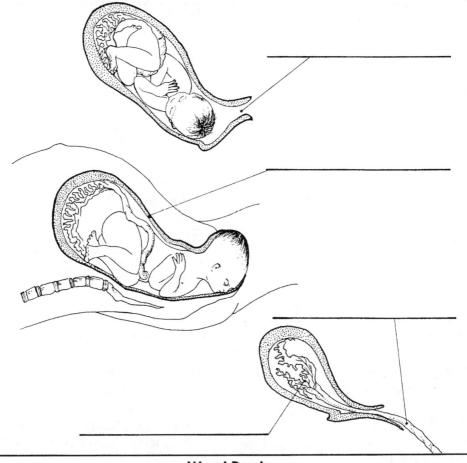

Word Bank

birth canal   placenta   uterus   umbilical cord

Organ Systems

Make an **X** in the correct box to show to which system/systems each organ belongs. One is done for you.

Organs	Systems						
	Diges-tive	Respi-ratory	Urinary	Repro-ductive	Circula-tory	Ner-vous	Endo-crine
Bladder			X				
Brain							
Heart							
Ovaries							
Liver							
Pancreas							
Kidneys							
Spinal Cord							
Lungs							
Small Intestines							
Diaphragm							
Mouth							
Nerves							
Testes							
Thyroid Gland							
Arteries							
Esophagus							
Cerebellum							

Feel the Beat

When the heart pumps, it forces blood out into the arteries. The walls of the arteries expand and contract to the rhythm of the heart which creates a **pulse**.

You can feel your pulse where the arteries are close to the surface of the skin. Two good places to feel a pulse are on the inside of the wrist, and on the neck to the side of the windpipe.

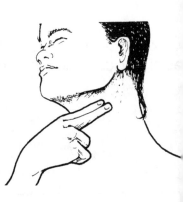

Try the experiments below and complete the chart by . . .

1. counting the number of heart beats in 15 seconds.
2. multiplying that number by 4 to get the pulse rate for one minute.

Study your results. Explain how each activity affected your pulse rate.

Activity	Pulse Rate for 15 sec.	X 4 =	Pulse Rate per minute
Sitting still for 10 minutes			
Running in place for 3 minutes.			
Just after finishing your lunch or dinner.			
While still in bed in the morning.			
Just after getting ready for school.			

Pressure Points

When a person is severely cut and begins to bleed, it's time for quick action. First aid for severe bleeding involves applying pressure over the wound. Sometimes it is possible to press the artery above the wound against the bone behind it, and stop the bleeding. This place is called a **pressure point**. A pressure point is also an excellent location to take a person's pulse.

Place an **X** on the pressure points listed in the Word Bank.

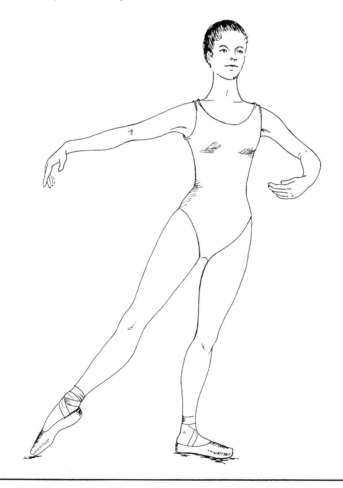

Word Bank

neck	behind the knee	inside the thigh
wrist	bend of elbow	top of foot

Name the Nutrient

Your body is made up of millions of cells that need food to stay alive. Your body needs **nutrients** from the foods you eat to help the cells grow and repair themselves. Nutrients are divided into six major groups: **fats, proteins, carbohydrates, minerals, vitamins** and **water**.

Read each clue. Identify these five nutrients.

"I'm the body's building material. You need me to make new tissue. You get plenty of me from milk, beans, meat, and peanuts."

Who am I? _____

"I give you energy to work and play. You can find me in starchy foods like pasta and potatoes."

Who am I? _____

"I help build strong bones and teeth. I also give you healthy red blood. You can find me in all four food groups."

Who am I? _____

"I give you a concentrated source of energy. You can find me in oily and greasy foods, like bacon, salad dressing, and butter. I also help you maintain healthy skin and hair."

Who am I? _____

"You might call me the alphabet soup of the nutrients. I am one of the essential nutrients. I don't give you energy, but I do help your body get energy from the other nutrients."

Who am I? _____

Word Bank
fat
protein
carbohydrate
vitamin
mineral

You Are What You Eat

Looking closely at the information on a cereal box you can learn many interesting things about the product.

Carefully read the information on this example from a cereal box. Answer the questions. Compare these answers with the information found on a box of cereal you might eat for breakfast.

	Corn Balls	Your Cereal
What kind of grain(s) is used?		
Is sugar used?		
What position is sugar on the list of ingredients?		
List other sweeteners.		
How many calories per serving without milk.		
How many calories per serving when eaten with 1/2 cup of skim milk?		
How much protein per serving?		
How many vitamins and minerals does the cereal contain?		
How much cholesterol is in one serving?		

NUTRITION INFORMATION

SERVING SIZE: 1 OZ. (28.4 g, ABOUT 1 CUP)
CORN BALLS ALONE OR WITH 1/2 CUP
VITAMINS A AND D SKIM MILK.
SERVINGS PER PACKAGE: 15

	CEREAL	WITH 1/2 CUP VITAMINS A & D SKIM MILK
CALORIES	110	150*
PROTEIN	1 g	5 g
CARBOHYDRATE	26 g	32 g
FAT	0 g	0 g*
CHOLESTEROL	0 mg	0 mg*
SODIUM	90 mg	150 mg
POTASSIUM	20 mg	220 mg

PERCENTAGE OF U.S. RECOMMENDED DAILY ALLOWANCES (U.S. RDA)

PROTEIN	2	10
VITAMIN A	15	20
VITAMIN C	25	25
THIAMIN	25	30
RIBOFLAVIN	25	35
NIACIN	25	25
CALCIUM	**	15
IRON	10	10
VITAMIN D	10	25
VITAMIN B_6	25	25
ZINC	10	15

* WHOLE MILK SUPPLIES AN ADDITIONAL 30
CALORIES. 4g. FAT, AND 15mg CHOLESTEROL.
** CONTAINS LESS THAN 2% OF THE U.S. RDA
OF THIS NUTRIENT.

INGREDIENTS: CORN, SUGAR, CORN
SYRUP, MOLASSES, SALT, ANNATTO
COLOR.

Reading the Label

The labels on medicine containers give us important information. Labels should always be read carefully.

Read the information on the cough medicine labels below. Answer the questions.

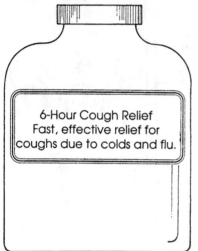

6-Hour Cough Relief
Fast, effective relief for
coughs due to colds and flu.

Recommended Dosage:
Children (5 - 12 years): 1 teaspoon every 6 hours.
Adults: 2 teaspoons every 6 hours.
Caution: Do not administer to children under 5. No more than 4 dosages per day. This product may cause drowsiness; use caution if operating machinery or driving a vehicle. Should not be taken if you are pregnant or nursing a child.
If cough or fever persists, consult a physician.
Exp. Date: 8/95

1. What is the adult dosage? _____

2. What is a child's dosage? _____

3. What is a side effect of this medicine? _____

4. Who should not take this medicine? _____
   _____

5. How many dosages per day can be taken safely? _____

6. What is the expiration date of this medicine? _____

7. What action should be taken if the medicine does not relieve your cough? _____
   _____

8. For what symptoms should this medicine be taken?
   _____

Caution: Poison!

Children are always very curious. They love to touch things and pick them up. Very young children like to put things into their mouths. What action do you take if a child swallows a poisonous material?

CALL YOUR POISON CONTROL CENTER, HOSPITAL, PHYSICIAN, OR EMERGENCY PHONE NUMBER IMMEDIATELY!

If you cannot obtain emergency advice, follow these procedures.

- If the poison is **corrosive:** paint remover, household cleaners, gasoline, drain opener, ammonia or lye, **DO NOT** make the patient vomit. Give the patient water or milk to dilute the poison.

- If the poison is **not corrosive:** insect spray, aspirin, pesticides or medicine, **make the patient vomit,** or use a poison control kit. To force the patient to vomit touch the back of his/her throat.

Write a bold "**V**" on each picture that shows poison that should be vomited if swallowed. **Circle** each poison that should **not** be vomited if swallowed.

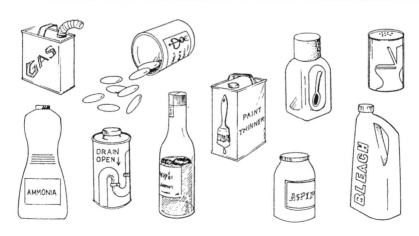

Human Body Review

Use the Word Bank to complete the puzzle.

Across:

1. outer layer of skin
4. the blood pump
6. stores urine
10. opening to the uterus
11. boney structure
12. the inside of the hand
13. controls body growth and other glands
16. a break in a bone
19. rhythm of the heart creates a _____
20. female sex glands

Down:

2. outer layer of the tooth
3. upper arm bone
5. gland that goes to work when we are excited, angry, or frightened
7. fluid surrounding fetus
8. long food tube
9. joint found in elbow
12. gland which controls the body's use of glucose
14. place by or beside a wound to stop bleeding
15. muscles are attached to the skeleton by _____
17. male sex glands
18. framework of bones that supports lower part of abdomen

Word Bank			
alimentary canal			
pressure point	heart	adrenal	ovaries	skeleton
pituitary	cervix	bladder	testes	fracture
epidermis	humerus	pulse	pelvis	tendons
palm	amniotic	hinge	pancreas	enamel